MW01152652

Hygge and Lagom

*The Ultimate Guide to Scandinavian Ways of
Living a Balanced Life Filled with Coziness
and Happiness*

Contents

Part 1: Hygge

Unlock the Danish Art of Coziness and Happiness

General Introduction

Cravings for comfort, coziness, and contentment: everyone experiences the desire for a happier, less stressful, and more serene life. Hygge, the Danish-born philosophy, is one proven way to achieve such a life. From the Old Norse for "well-being", hygge embodies a philosophy that is as much a mindset as it is a way of life with specific activities designed to encourage you to cultivate togetherness and joy at the smallest and simplest things in everyday life.

With this book, you will learn about the hygge lifestyle, with a philosophical overview of what hygge is and how it relates to overall happiness. The Danes have been voted happiest people on earth numerous times; surely, this homegrown philosophy has something of merit to recommend it. Also, within the book are many basic tips and ideas for how to practice hygge in your own life, from home décor and atmosphere to how you dress and spend your leisure time. There is also a hygge way of approaching food and entertainment, the holidays, and seasonal activities. Underlying it all, hygge continually emphasizes the spirit of togetherness, fostering relationships with family and friends, and nurturing yourself through self-care.

Simplicity and serenity go hand-in-hand to create an atmosphere of cozy comfort and genuine fellowship. So, go find yourself a pair of warm, woolen socks, a super-soft blanket, and curl up in a hyggekrog (cozy nook). Read on about how to immerse yourself in hygge, the Danish secret to a happier life!

Chapter 1 Introduction: What the Heck is Hygge?

Consistently ranked among the happiest - if not the most joyful - nations on earth, Denmark must be doing something right. All human beings crave comfort, security, and happiness; indeed, the pursuit of happiness is one of the defining motivations of modern life. The Danes seem to have stumbled upon a simple secret that the rest of us - with our busy, distracted lives - have missed. That little secret well-being might be a concept called *hygge*. Pronounced "hoo-gah," hygge describes a lifestyle filled with contentment, a kind of "coziness of the soul," according to Meik Wiking, the CEO of the Happiness Research Institute in Copenhagen. Hygge encompasses a wide range of attitudes, feelings, and activities that are designed for comfort and happiness in security and simplicity.

Where Does Hygge Come From?

Various sources suggest different origins for the word "hygge," though all agree that it has some relation to comfort and coziness. Most sources suggest that the word originated from the Norwegian - with whom the Danes shared a nation-state until the early nineteenth century. To Norwegians, it means "well-being." It is also translated from the Danish to mean "to give courage, comfort, joy," and it has become a defining characteristic of Danish culture, particularly in the last few years. In 2016, it was in the finals for "word of the year" according to the *Oxford English Dictionary*, and there has been an explosion of interest in the concept and lifestyle that it defines. One could speculate that the timing is no accident, given the uncertainties in international politics and the continuing growth of technology often perceived as alienating.

In another line of etymological thinking, hygge may be derived from the sixteenth-century word *hugge* which means "to embrace," which is also linked to the words *hygga*, meaning "to comfort," and *hugr*, meaning "mood." Whatever the exact origin of the term, hygge has come to mean a combination of all the above: a warm, embracing hug as a way of life.

What about those Woolen Socks?

Hygge is defined by numerous characteristics, from the way your home is decorated and lit to the comfort in your personal attire. In fact, lighting is one of the key components of implementing the hygge atmosphere into your life: more than three-quarters of Danes, when asked what they most associate with hygge, say "candles." From this, you can infer that one of the most important characteristics of hygge is the attention to home and hearth. Indeed, the emphasis on togetherness and social relationships is also key to hygge, and your hyggelige home should be warm and welcoming, with the soothing glow of candlelight.

Still, hygge is not merely about the comforts of home (though this is crucial); it is also about how you eat and drink, dress, and celebrate. Simple and hearty food, without too much fuss, is a hallmark of the hygge lifestyle. Hygge doesn't demand that you count calories obsessively or that you put too many nutritional expectations on yourself. Conversely, it doesn't indicate that you can indulge just for the sake of indulgence - that's not the hygge way. Instead, hygge embraces simple moderation combined with a sense of calm and comfort. Stew and porridge factor largely in the pleasures of hygge, along with warming drinks and general relaxation. A decent blanket and a pair of soothing woolen socks are must-haves for an evening in front of a fire, or the glow of a television set, not to eliminate all the trappings of modernity. A "Netflix and chill" evening may not be the most central tenant of hygge, though its aim is far off the mark! Clothing is comfortable and basic, practical, and cozy. Hygge is not about "seeing and being seen," or standing out in a crowd; it is a humble way of presenting yourself to the world, with your happiness illuminating you from the inside out. The same attitude applies to celebrations: celebrate with contentment and togetherness, embracing your gratitude toward all the little things that make up your good life.

Hygge and Mindfulness

Once you begin to embrace hygge, it becomes not only a style but also a mindset. It encourages you to see the world differently, not through what you can acquire or achieve but through how you can appreciate and take part in the *small joys of life*. As with the Eastern concepts of mindfulness and meditation, hygge encourages you to stay in the present, enjoying what you have with loved ones and spending your time qualitatively rather than quantitatively. Indeed, this may be one of the central components of the hygge lifestyle that defines the contemporary Danish understanding of happiness: decoupling the feelings of happiness and comfort from the trappings of wealth and status.

This is part of the idea of hygge, as well, which also emphasizes equality and teamwork, modesty and simplicity. Some criticize this spirit within the Scandinavian culture in general, suggesting that it encourages a kind of conformity long associated with various Northern European countries. This conformity welcomes the idea that no particular person should stand out or show off. While hygge may suggest an element of this thought, it by no means encourages it as the aim of the lifestyle. Rather, it encourages finding satisfaction in the everyday parts of life, promoting tolerance and togetherness that everyone should be a part of.

State-sponsored Hygge

The argument about what makes hygge so achievable in Danish life - and its similar cousins in other Nordic countries - lies within the success of the so-called "welfare state." Many of the financial burdens of middle-class life in Danish society are relieved via the state: universal health care, social security, free education at universities, plenty of paid family leave and generous paid vacation time, as well as a highly functional infrastructure. Thus, Danes can enjoy the small comforts of life and the inherent joys of family and friends because they are not ridden with anxiety over how to afford a decent, comfortable middle-class existence. That said, Danish taxes are quite high (especially when compared to America), hovering above 50 percent in personal income tax. Still, the Danes are quite willing to accept this tax rate in exchange for the excellent benefits. Their priorities center around investing in the quality of life and participating in the larger society, a kind of culture of national togetherness - something other Western countries might seriously consider.

Hygge is most definitely associated with a level of financial security and economic mobility that many other places and peoples in the world do not have. This is part of what makes the practice of hygge special in its attributes - but rare in its attainability.

The spirit of hygge emphasizes humility in its practice. Having a secure social system and a stable infrastructure provides great assistance in attaining the highest levels of hyggelige. Still, regardless of the availability of that assistance, you can indulge in the daily mindset of embracing the simplicity of every day, the comforting and familial of nearly any circumstance. Again, hygge is not merely a set of rules;' it is a mindset devoted to engaging with daily life in a present, mindful, and positive manner.

The Most Hyggelige Time of the Year

Unsurprisingly, wintertime (especially Christmas) is when hygge is intensely recognized and practiced by those in Nordic lands. The reasons are numerous: in a harsh winter climate, it makes perfect sense to bask in the warm comforts of cozy, woolen socks and gently roaring fires, wrapped in a blanket in a candlelit room. Foods and drinks most associated with a hygge lifestyle are also all about warming comfort: porridges, and stews and mulled wines. These are all welcome distractions from the raging winter weather outside - and more than that, they are all reminders of how our own little pocket of daily life is safe and warm, cozy, and comforting. We create a shelter from all of life's storms.

This is not to say that hygge cannot be practiced year-round – of course, it should - but it also acknowledges that festive spirit that comes with most winter holidays. For many of us who celebrate Christmas, this festive spirit is quite familiar and very similar to many of the aspects of hygge itself. A hygge lifestyle is lived in this festive spirit, evoked throughout the year, encouraged by taking pleasure in intimate surroundings with our loved ones *every day*, not just snow days! Indeed, we would all be much happier looking forward to – and building our days around - an appreciation of daily life, togetherness, and cozy contemplation - no matter the time of year.

Practicing Hygge

So, now that you have a solid understanding of what hygge is and why it deserves careful consideration as a lifestyle, let's talk about how this can work for you in practical ways.

In the next chapter, we will examine the direct link between personal happiness and the practice of hygge: what is happiness, and how can hygge be a conduit to achieving it? Then, we will move on to exploring the practical ways in which we can integrate the concept of hygge into most aspects of our lives.

From the general attitude of employing hygge into our everyday lives to the fine details of how to practice particular parts of hyggelige, the rest of the book will look at specific elements of life in which hygge plays an important role. Creating a home environment that encourages and supports the mindset of hygge is key, as well as considering your personal dress and appearance; nothing too fussy, but certainly something lovely and comfortable. There are also tips and techniques - along with a handful of recipes - for cooking and consuming in the hygge style, with another chapter specifically focused on how to hygge up your holidays at any time of the year.

Following that, we will look at how hygge can increase our happiness by amplifying our familial relationships. Areas include using hygge in parenting, as well as bringing our loved ones together in positive ways for more sustained periods of time. We will also address the frugal nature of hygge; it is not a lifestyle that is based on conspicuous consumption and ambitious striving. Rather, it is a gentle, peaceful, and comfortable existence that can be achieved with little in the way of material struggling. Finally, we will spend some time looking at hygge-styled crafts and how we can engage in creating a cozier life with our own two hands.

Unlock this uniquely Danish art of living happily and cozily, embracing life with an open, warm hug, and engaging with your world in a mindful, humble manner. Happiness and well-being are only a few chapters away!

Chapter 2: How Hygge Helps Happiness

While it is our inalienable right to pursue happiness here in the US, too often it feels elusive considering our hectic, harried lifestyles and attachments to too many material things. Hygge may be one way to right that ship, supported with clear evidence from Denmark being consistently considered the happiest country on earth. Possibly, some guidance from the hygge lifestyle is just what we need to help guide us to greater happiness.

We all want bliss and happiness, and our ideas of that - and for that - vary from one person to another. For many of us, there are points in our life that disappoint; we thought we were on the path to happiness just to find we weren't even close to the right direction! We wind up very unhappy instead. Many studies have shown that people choosing to follow the high dollar, high-stress careers end up less content than peers who chose rewarding careers helping their fellow man - even if less financially lucrative. This is where a concept like hygge can come in and reframe our concepts of happiness. Instead of being defined by wealth and achievement, it may be marked by family togetherness and a contented home. If what we once thought we wanted has failed to bring happiness, then surely there are alternate ways of defining happiness. Hygge is demonstrably one of them, as people who practice it routinely report high levels of happiness and contentment.

Happiness as a destination for solely our personal fulfillment should not be the only thing driving us. Living a joyful life is also crucial to our overall health and well-being, emotionally and physically. The medical evidence keeps mounting: unhappiness is detrimental to our short-term needs and our long-term health. Among other things, it promotes heart health. People reporting happiness also report lower blood pressure and heart rates, both of which affect long-term heart health. It also boosts our immune systems; people who consistently maintained positive outlooks on their lives also consistently avoided colds and other minor ailments over time! In fact, happiness helps us to avoid pain in general - people who claim to be happy report far fewer aches and pains that many of us experience in our daily lives. The difference here may not be necessarily physical, but it is no less powerful to contemplate that our state of mind can alleviate physical pain itself. Other, more complicated diseases have shown to be less severe or to occur less often in people who reported spending a lot of time in social groups. Certainly, high levels of happiness are associated with low levels of stress, and we have all heard of how acutely damaging stress is to our physical well-being over time. Last, happy people often lead longer lives and are more productive well into their later years. The benefits of feeling happiness are undeniable, and, like hygge, this is a state of mind. The Danes are a great example of hygge in action!

Many wellness experts tout the benefits of the hygge lifestyle in its improvement over our emotional state of mind, our physical health, and our social well-being. Emotionally, one of the benefits of hygge is to promote a sense of calm and peacefulness. For example, if your home is cozy and comforting - with gentle candlelit rooms, warm furniture, blankets, and the smells of delicious home cooking - then it stands to reason that your state of mind is also at peace, not stressful. Other emotional benefits of hygge practice may include a decrease in depression - it's hard to stay depressed when you're comfortable and secure without much anxiety. Additionally, increased feelings of optimism and self-worth are often by-products of practicing hygge, as your state of mind will not be as linked to external desires and things that may be out of your control. This will also foster a sense of mindfulness and an appreciation for the little things in your life. Living a life filled with gratitude is certainly a sign of living a life filled with happiness.

As discussed above, practicing hygge in your life leads to physical health benefits. In addition to the emotional benefits, the physical benefits are just as important. Incorporating hygge into your daily routine can lead to a physically stronger life. For instance, hygge can improve sleep patterns - crucial to maintaining a sense of calm productivity. Within the security of a hygge space, external threats no longer loom large, and with that comfort comes better sleep, which leads to better self-care overall. It is difficult, for example, to exercise regularly and maintain a healthy weight if one is depressed, anxious, and lacking sleep. Also, some suggest that practicing hygge keeps you from overindulging in substances that allegedly help you cope with stress but can harm you physically, such as alcohol or other drugs.

Finally, there are also social benefits gained from practicing hygge. When we feel safe and comfortable, it becomes easier to reach out to others without feeling insecure and vulnerable. If we make our home welcoming and inviting to ourselves, it follows that others will find out home equally as alluring.

One of the fundamental concepts within hygge is that togetherness is truly part of the formula for overall happiness. Connecting with others is important both for our personal well-being and that of our community. This is an art that is being lost in the maze of technological devices and the distractions of our contemporary world. We may like using the word "communication" when discussing our beloved technology of texting or social media, yet our devices don't foster an authentic sense of connection. Hygge can help us to regain some of that feeling of connection. When a sense of security and comfort is established and maintained, we can then focus on increasing our trust in one another, ultimately creating a greater sense of intimacy within our relationships in general. Getting away from social media and instead focusing on sociability in your home and in your activities goes a long way toward fostering a long-term sense of well-being. Human beings are social animals, after all, and working to improve those social relationships is certainly part of the recipe for achieving lasting happiness.

Achieving happiness through hygge involves focusing on creating a cozy space and a comforting lifestyle; this facilitates and nurtures happier feelings. For example, if your home is a space of refuge - a calm, shared space with a warm fire, decorated with soothing natural materials - then you are likely to feel protected, safe, and calm. We will explore more about how to create this kind of ideal space in Chapter 4.

The application of hygge in your life boils down to a few key features, all of which will be discussed at greater length in the following chapters. These are crucial elements to letting hygge into your life: warm lighting, such as candlelight, is perhaps the most important element in igniting the hygge spirit in your home. Texture in clothing (or anything touching your skin) is also important, as all things soft and warm are key to promoting a calm and relaxed environment. Think cozy socks or a soft throw. The décor in your home also plays a role in promoting hygge, with the use of natural elements taking precedence over the cold, hard surfaces of glass and steel. This also applies to the use of color: neutral, warm colors are more inviting than bold, overwhelming ones. Beige and cream, with light hints of color, is more calming than bright reds, yellows, or oranges. Obviously, hygge - coming from a cold, northern clime - is also all about warmth, but not just regarding room temperature. Internal, psychological warmth is a result of providing a safe and comfortable environment for everyone who enters your space -

yourself included. An inviting space is a harmonious space. Also, think about how you arrange your space: togetherness is a key component of hygge, and people within that space should feel connected and comforted by each other as well as their environment.

Activities suggested by the hygge lifestyle all reflect tenants described above. This is not about hosting formal dinners or leading loud rounds of competitive games. It could be anything from simple conversation to a home-style dinner to coffee and cards at the end of an evening. Whatever you plan in your space, attune it to the goal of togetherness and connection with your family and friends.

Last, don't limit yourself to practicing hygge just in your home or on your days off. This is a lifestyle that takes time to cultivate, carrying with it the worthwhile goal of improving your happiness, health, and well-being. Implement some of these strategies at your place of employment when possible and appropriate. Reflect on the benefits of walking into an office with soft lighting, personal and pleasant pictures, with perhaps a plant of two. That office is infinitely more inviting than one with harsh overhead lights and nothing more personal than a desktop computer. Think about a mental health professional's office; most are purposefully designed to comfort and soothe the patients who enter there. This can also be your purpose at work, putting clients or others at ease as well as lowering your own levels of stress.

Think about other ways to cultivate the hygge spirit throughout your daily activities. Communing with nature, rather than zoning out with our technological devices, is one sure way to practice the habit of hygge. Take a leisurely bike ride and walk along the trails to experience the natural world; be present and unhurried in how you approach activity. The goal is to feel calm and peaceful, not frantic and competitive. Slow down a bit: the contemporary American lifestyle is geared to go at lightning speed, and this often means we miss out on the little joys, such as listening to birdsong or watching a sunset. You can also think of hygge as a way to do good in the world, albeit in small, incremental ways. Practice sustainability for the greater common good. Recycling, eating locally produced foods, and seeking out environmentally friendly power sources are all activities that adhere to the overall spirit of hygge.

You can also carry hygge with you throughout your day via your attitude, your way of presenting yourself, your way of connecting with others - even strangers. In the next chapter, we will explore the many little things that can make up our peaceful day while practicing hygge.

Chapter 3: Practical Hygge: How to Have a Danish Day

While most Americans begin and end their days in a dead run:

- gulping coffee and -if you're lucky – breakfast
- getting the kids to school
- dodging traffic
- making it to work on time
- catching up on emails
- work-work-work
- getting kids to activities
- rushing home
- eating take-out or leftovers on the go
- collapsing into bed

This clearly the opposite of how to have a Danish day! The emphasis is not on accomplishing tasks or ticking off items on a list; the emphasis is on living a present and happy life. Instead of focusing on instant gratification or realizing consumerist fantasies, the Danes seek to experience relationships with people and their environment. Let's imagine how we might immerse ourselves in a Danish day of hygge: simple, practical, interactive, *and happy*.

Good Morning!

After a wonderfully well-rested night, you wake up to light the candles around the house, giving off a soft, warm glow that brings you gently into the day. The house is neat and simple, organized but comfortable, with just enough of what you need without the clutter of conspicuous consumption. Make a generous cup of cocoa - or rich, dark coffee - and have a slice of dense, comforting rugbrød (Danish rye bread). Or, perhaps a big bowl of porridge is more appropriate to fuel your day, complete with whole grains, some sliced fruit and a handful of chopped nuts sprinkled over it all. If it's a weekday, get ready to go to your workspace for five or six hours. Greet your colleagues warmly - for they are friends - and finish your work without fear of missing out on home life, because you will be seeing your family this evening.

If you are Danish, you are most likely working in a position that affords you a solid and stable life. Remember, a Dane's post-high school education is free, leading to a workplace that is less competitive and more collaborative. Remember that work should be a place that fulfills your need to be creative. We should all be productive, contributing to the world around us, and because we are only concerned with amassing money or status! In Denmark, the gap between the wealthy and the not-so-wealthy is the lowest in the world; everyone has the chance to live a secure and contented life. If you were to lose your job, then the government would help you out - up to 90 percent of your paycheck would be provided for about four years as a cushion until you found another opportunity. Work is satisfying because it is a career of choice, and your workspace is nearly as inviting as your home. It doesn't feel like drudgery because it is not the only important thing in your life, as your supervisor and your colleagues well know! Work is one part of a full life, and you do not take it home with you. Instead, you leave in the afternoon, ready to enjoy the rest of what life has to offer.

Good Afternoon

It is afternoon, and that is the perfect time to spend some of it outdoors. At home, you have large windows that allow you to bask in the sunlight during the long summer days or revel in the snow and storms that carry on during the short winter days. Each day, you plan to spend some time outside in the fresh air, communing with nature. Perhaps you decide to go to the park, where you will invariably run into someone you know, a friend perhaps or a neighbor. Maybe you will meet them there for an afternoon picnic if the weather cooperates. No matter: Danish weather is always unpredictable, but you are always prepared. A picnic in the park could just as easily become an afternoon spent in a café. You'll probably spend time with friends in the café in any case. It's the Danish thing to do!

You hop on your bike - nine out of ten Danes have one, often using them daily - getting exercise that doesn't feel like exercise while you amble over to the café. You've already had your simple lunch - some smørrebrød of liver pâté, herring or roast pork. Now, the café is time for a nice cup of coffee or cocoa and, of course, a lovely sweet, perhaps a pastry or a big slice of cake. Fulfilling sweets are definitely a part of practical hygge - all that walking and biking and communing with nature gives you more reason to indulge. You meet with some friends, a nice intimate group of three or four where you can talk about your work, the weather, the kids, whatever strikes your fancy. The important part of each day is socializing and being together with your friends. One of your friends brings her newborn in a stroller, and since the weather is nice, you all sit outside while you share thoughts and coffee and cake. Your friend is enjoying her generous maternity leave; she gets a very fulfilling full year to spend with her child before she returns to work. Everyone shares in this humane opportunity to nurture a newborn, a perk of the Danish social welfare system.

Once you have finished your leisurely café break, it is off to the market, where you go to purchase some fresh produce and other ingredients for the evening meal. This is a significant part of the day, something that you do most days because cooking and eating together is a very important part of daily life. In addition, the practice of hygge emphasizes fostering local relationships and contributing to the good in the world: shopping at the market is an excellent way to fulfill all these elements. You build relationships with the farmers, the proprietors, and you buy the healthiest and freshest food that you can find to nurture yourself and your family. It's not about fancy and fussy ingredients, but rather fresh and wholesome ones for the simple meal that you will prepare - with the help of your partner or family or friends - for supper that night.

When you get home from your forays, you decide to take a little time for self-care. Perhaps you light some candles in the bathroom and take a soothing bath before preparing the evening meal. If it's summer, perhaps you sit outside with another cup of coffee and enjoy the afternoon sunlight with the paper or a puzzle, or you simply spend some time relaxing with your own thoughts. Go ahead; this is what the hyggelige is all about. It takes some re-charging to re-energize! If it's winter, perhaps you make a fire and wrap yourself in a blanket in your cozy hyggekrog (hygge corner) and pick up a good book to read. Whatever you decide, it is never a bad idea to spend some time in self-care, treating yourself to some calming moments of your own choosing. Once you are re-charged, you'll be ready and eager for some family and friend time.

Good Evening

Now you are ready to begin preparing the evening meal. The family is all at home by now - everyone knows that the evening meal is to be spent together and that friends are always welcome - and everyone of age contributes to the preparation and presentation of the meal. Because this is a typical Danish day, you have decided to make something hearty and healthy, simple but full of comforting flavor. Perhaps you have decided to make stegtflaesk, one of the national dishes of the Danes, consisting of some crispy pork and boiled potatoes with parsley-cream sauce. Or, perhaps you are just channeling the spirit of hygge and decide to make an earthy stew with some meat and vegetables that you bought at the market - something simple that requires just a bit of time to prepare, then a nice while to cook whilst filling the house with comforting aromas. This gives you time to talk with family and friends, make a warming drink or two, and set the table so that everyone feels welcome and comfortable. Certainly, setting the atmosphere is one of the key aspects of hygge, and you like to present a table with some nice tableware and/or flowers and/or decorative vases. The focus is not about the objects themselves, but rather about making the table an inviting and pleasant place to want to gather around. Of course, everyone has turned off their phones and set aside their tablets or laptops, because this is all about spending quality time together.

Once dinner is ready, everyone gathers and eats, family-style, relishing the simple pleasures of dining together on good, fresh food that is prepared in the home and eaten as a family. This may be one of the most crucial pieces to the puzzle of Danish happiness: this kind of special family time isn't saved for special occasions at all. These times are everyday events, fostering a culture of kindness, generosity, and gratitude. One could even suggest that the high rates of happiness and low rates of poverty and crime are borne of the simple fact that breaking bread together is one of the most powerful unifiers within any society. Some would say that once that is lost, there is a kind of fellowship that is sorely missed. Hence, the Danish emphasis on work-life balance is so deeply ingrained in the culture. Danes feel that you are not truly living without having this unifying time spent with loved ones, fostering meaningful relationships, and sharing your life with others.

After dinner, as darkness falls - in summer, this will be late; in winter, dusk comes quite early - you gather in your cozy space, with intimate room for all. Perhaps you decide to play some friendly games together, or it is time for casual conversation. If you and your partner or spouse are on your own, you may decide to watch a film together, snuggled in a warm blanket in front of a fire or bathed in candlelight. Perhaps you are on your own for the evening, which gives you the chance to return to your hyggekrog and spend a glorious couple of hours reading a wonderful book. Because your day has been spent enjoying each moment without stress and hurry or the feeling that you never have time to accomplish enough, you fall asleep easily and dream lightly of another beautiful hyggelige day.

The Takeaway

Hygge itself is nearly undefinable in English: for some, it indicates a lifestyle, as loosely outlined above; for others, it indicates a personal feeling of cozy comfort. For others, it indicates a mindset of being present in each moment of the day. Basically, the combination of all three will get you closest to the experience of hygge in a typical Danish day. The reason for hygge's recent popularity seems to need little explanation: in a harried world of stress and demands, hygge represents a return to something that is simpler, happier, and ultimately more fulfilling.

Certainly, Danish society is set up for hygge, with its generous welfare state, equal and stable wages, and a cultural penchant for work-life balance. Not only do Danes have the shortest workweek in Europe (around 35 hours for most), but they also are afforded at least five weeks of paid vacation a year, and mothers have paid maternity leave for a full year. There are also social safety nets of all kinds, from free education through university to unemployment benefits that pay up to 90 percent of your salary for up to four years. Extreme poverty and homelessness are virtually unknown throughout Denmark, and health care is nationalized and free. All of this comes at the cost of taxpayers, of course, and Danes pay the highest tax rates of just about any country in the world (close to 60 percent in 2019). Still, most Danes do not complain about the high tax rate because of the social benefits that everyone receives. It is a rare instance of a truly egalitarian society wherein most people believe that their country will be better off if everyone were educated, healthy, and taken care of when necessary.

When we look around at other Western countries, particularly America, we see a vast gap between the very wealthy and the very poor, something which doesn't exist in Denmark. The trade-off, as some would argue, is that you don't really have the opportunity to get rich in Denmark; everyone is educated, salaries are comparable across the board. Elevating your own status is not easily done. A typical Danish response might be to suggest that happiness does not equate with wealth or status. Danes have little to fear from crime or other ills that societies with great wealth inequality face. These are just a few societal norms that give Danes little reason to change their present system.

If you are a woman in Danish society, then you might even have a more beneficial view of this system. For many reasons, Danish women do not feel pressure to get married. Their society is so egalitarian; women have as much education and opportunity as men. They have access to the same kinds of stable, well-paying jobs. Women do not have to rely on men for money or status. Second, with the generous maternity leave and unemployment benefits, women can achieve a much greater balance between work and life, especially regarding having and raising a family. This is one of the most important aspects of Danish culture that other Western countries would do well to consider. Third, shifting the emphasis away from marriage as a transactional relationship means that it can become a more emotionally satisfying one; you can focus on fostering a relationship rather than achieving a contractual marriage.

So, Danish societal systems are set up in line with the practice of hygge! Living elsewhere, many do not necessarily enjoy the benefits and security of that particular national way of life. If the hygge way of life appears to you, it is still possible to introduce elements of hygge into your daily routine with thoughtfulness and care. Who isn't drawn to a life of less stress, more mindfulness, and cozy contentment? This is what starting to practice hygge requires: a desire to create an atmosphere conducive to comfort and calm, a focus on togetherness and family rather than work and status, and a belief that material wealth and consumer products do not equal happiness. Rather, it is an intrinsic feeling that comes from leading a comforting life of self-care and well-being. There are many ways to achieve this mindset and practice this lifestyle, and the following chapters will give you many specific ideas of how to introduce this Danish experience into your life.

The Checklist

✓ Self-care is the key! Hygge is about giving yourself permission to set down all your stresses and worries and making sure that you are healthy and happy - only then can you help others be happy and healthy, as well.

✓ Atmosphere cements the mindset. Soft lighting - most Danes agree that without candlelight, there can be no hyggelige. It is a must - along with earthy and comforting décor, big windows when possible, simplicity of design and a minimum of clutter. Less stuff equals more life.

✓ Simplicity, simplicity, simplicity! Hygge is all about appreciating the simple pleasures in life: get outdoors, talk with friends, spend time in a café, read a good book, stay in the present, and appreciate what you have.

✓ Speaking of the outdoors, get out there every day. Fresh air and wholesome exercise – riding a bike or playing in the park - are also crucial to cultivating the practice of hygge. Nature should be an inspiration to enjoy daily.

✓ Café culture is important all over Europe, but it is certainly a huge part of the hygge lifestyle. This is about being with friends, enjoying warming drinks and tasty (read: sugary) foods. Cafés are central to the Danish day.

✓ Markets are also significant. Kitchens are small and spare in much of Europe in general, and daily shopping at the local market is a way of life for many. It's a way to commune with others, to contribute to the community, and to provide healthy local food and goods for your family.

✓ Prepare dinner at home and eat together - *every day* – or at least as often as is practically possible. Turn off phones and other devices and make each evening a gathering that's worthy of a holiday season.

✓ Success is not defined via one material thing. Rather, success is about work-life balance, creativity, and productivity in your life, comfort, and happiness in your home.

Chapter 4: Practical Hygge: Hygge Your House

If you've ever encountered Old Norse mythology or traditional Scandinavian poetry, you will encounter one overarching theme: the absolute inviolable importance of the security and sanctity of home and hearth. In *Beowulf*, a famous old tale involving Danes and Swedes and probably the most famous embraced by English-speakers, our hero must combat the ravages that the beast Grendel has perpetrated on the great hall of Heorot. Grendel's sin is to flout the unbreakable conventions of hospitality and to violate the safe haven that is the home and hearth of King Hrothgar's great peoples.

This social law of hospitality runs deep within Scandinavian culture, the remnant of a time when harsh winters and poor harvests could leave people homeless and starving. You are never to turn a stranger away, and you welcome all with the greatest of hospitality, no matter how humble your offerings.

While hygge itself is a more recent - and perhaps more modulated - take on the importance of home and hearth, the general rules of hospitality apply. It is linked to a long and lasting tradition in which the most important social interactions take place in a warm and safe environment wherein food and drink - and stories - are shared. Out of this, modern Danes have embraced hygge, with its emphasis on simple pleasures and café culture, the togetherness of people, and the fostering of happiness on self-care and social interaction – not material goods.

Not only is hygge a state of mind wherein you create a feeling of well-being and comfort, but it also encompasses a particular visual style and atmospheric component that assists in the overall feeling of contentment. In recent years, designers and other influencers have promoted the Danish look in home décor and in entertainment venues, and this is easy to replicate in your home. "Hygge-fying" your house is important if you truly want to change your lifestyle, as your home is your primary place of experience. There are many ways in which you can personalize your hygge home, of course, but the following are some guidelines for the elements that are most important in unlocking a hygge-inspired sense of comfort and happiness.

Whole House Hygge

There are certain elements of hygge style that are relevant and welcome in any space in the home. Some of these elements have to do with creating an overall atmosphere of welcome, warmth, comfort, and coziness, while others are about creating a look that supports the atmosphere you are trying to achieve. It cannot be overstated how important it is to "hygge your house up" if you want to live a hygge life; the comfort and centrality of home and hearth is one of the central tenants in this Danish philosophy.

> o **Lighting**: this is one of the most crucial elements to creating a hygge atmosphere in your home. As mentioned in the beginning chapters, most Danes see a direct link between candles and hygge - indeed; many say that, without candles, there can be no hygge home spirit. Thus, what many Americans might see as a fire hazard is essential to this way

of life in Denmark. Just exercise common sense and a dose of caution when placing and lighting candles throughout your home, and you should have no problems. Aside from candles, think about accent lighting - small lamps in corners of rooms; dimmer switches for larger spaces - rather than harsh, overhead lighting. Natural light is also warm and inviting, depending on the time of year and angle of the sun; in hygge homes, windows are generally large and uncovered to allow for the natural world to glow within the home. As we all know from dining out or snuggling up with a date on the couch, lighting is key to setting a mood; the mood that you want to set in your hygge home is one of soothing comfort. Soft lighting should be the rule of the day throughout the home.

o **Other visual elements**: color is also important to the hygge home, with an emphasis on neutral, serene colors that serve to complement the soft, natural lighting and contribute to the soothing sensibility of the home. Look out for too much embellishment, which distracts from the overall effect of coziness.

o **Music**: almost as crucial as lighting in terms of setting a mood, what we listen to often impacts how we feel about the world around us. This might mean that in your hygge home, silence is best in order to allow the sounds of nature to carry through if you live in a rural area or are vacationing in a cabin in the woods). If you live in a bustling city or a crowded building, setting mood music throughout the home is an excellent way to enhance the hygge atmosphere. Again, the emphasis is on soothing comfort, rather than rousing loudness; perhaps classical music fits your style, or soft jazz, or simple instrumentals. Check the volume, too; this should be background music, not a distraction from the conversation and activities with family and friends.

o **Warmth**: this is also a key element within a hygge home, which makes perfect sense if you come from a northern clime. Denmark has famously cold and long winters, so hygge must have been developed, in part, to deal with this kind of climactic onslaught. It's also psychologically potent, the idea of refuge in the middle of the storm, that all of us can relate to no matter where we come from. A haven in the middle of tumultuous weather is a trope that we encounter in literature as far back as Homer and his *Odyssey*. Aside from that, the idea of welcome is emphasized by warmth. For these reasons, be sure to check temperatures throughout your home, seeing to it that everyone who visits feels warm (shorthand for welcomed and secure). Also, think of providing blankets - not just on beds but also around the home - as a kind of useable décor, providing warmth and comfort wherever a person may choose to wander.

o **Create Hyggekrogs**: there should be a comfortable and cozy nook in every home, and ideally, your hygge home will have more than one or two. A cushion and blanket in front of the fireplace, a window seat in the bedroom, a divan in the office for reading, or a sunroom with a rocking chair. These are all quiet places where you, your family, or your friends can curl up with a good book or a journal or a simple mug of coffee and your own thoughts. These little nooks should be cozied-up with blankets, cushions, and soft lighting to accommodate anyone's daily self-care.

o **Nice Smells**: anyone who remembers visits to their grandparents' home might well remember the cozy smell of baking bread or cookies or pie. If you are lucky, these scents remind you of your own home growing up. If a home is lit beautifully and decorated with care, it matters little if it doesn't also have a lovely smell to go with it. As anyone who has read Proust knows, scent triggers our strongest memories, and this atmospheric element should not be forgotten. Short of baking bread or pastries, you could arrange flowers or plants throughout the house, making sure that they aren't overpowering or allergy-causing. There are many natural scents available to add an alluring touch to space. Again, the key here is subtlety; too much scent is an irritation, and too many competing scents become a distraction.

o **Natural Décor**: when choosing your décor for your hygge home, focus on using natural elements such as wood, dried flowers, stone, and other items straight from nature. One of the emphases within hygge living is to respect and enjoy nature, so using natural elements in your décor keeps within that tenant. This is also an excellent way to practice another Danish habit: recycling. Danes are frugal in the sense that it is frowned upon to let anything go to waste, so re-using old bits and pieces of natural materials is certainly within the hygge spirit. This is also in the spirit of de-emphasizing consumer culture, as many elements of Danish décor could easily be "found" items: pebbles from the local lake fill a jar on the sideboard table; flowers from the field behind the house are dried to fill a vase at the table; seeds and beans are layered in mason jars to display in the kitchen. Embrace what is imperfect and look at old objects in a different way; there is much beauty to be found in trinkets and keepsakes you already have in your possession. Use your imagination and your location to determine how to put together your own personalized hygge home. Think about the color scheme, as well, using natural and neutral colors rather than bright, overbearing ones.

o **Texture in Décor**: another consideration when adding items to beautify your hygge home is to add layers of texture. The most important texture in the hygge spirit is that of softness - warm socks, cozy blankets, smooth sheets - but when layered with a bit of variety, texture can dress up the minimalist Danish look in clean and subtle ways. Again, stick to natural elements when thinking of texture, such as leather and wool or woods of different grains; use a healthy dose of restraint, as a hygge home is a minimalist home.

o **Neatness**: another key to creating a hygge home that is welcoming to all is to keep it neat and tidy; clutter detracts from the soothing atmosphere that you've worked so hard to achieve, as well as takes away from your focus on living life rather than accumulating stuff. A hygge home is by no means an austere home, with sharp edges and sparse spaces. It is, in fact, quite the opposite, with inviting blankets and comforting corners in which to curl up. It is also clean and neat without extraneous material to interrupt the interactions among others or your calming rituals of self-care.

Living Area

The most important thing to remember about your living area is that it is the heart of the home (alongside the kitchen), and there is a reason why the terms "home and hearth" go together: most ideal hygge homes will have a fireplace. It provides warmth and soft lighting, as well as a reminder of nature within the home itself. But do not despair if you live in a hearth-less home: make your own. It is undoubtedly cheating to put on a virtual image of a flickering fire on the television set. However, if this is an option, it shouldn't be dismissed. Even a virtual fire can help to create an atmosphere of warmth. Seeing and hearing a fire creates a Pavlovian response in most, triggering sensations of warmth and comfort regardless of the fire's reality. Certainly, gas log fireplaces create that illusion. Fire is also quite symbolic across all cultures, representing warmth and symbolizing fellowship, food, the cooking of meat, and breaking of bread. It brings both light and life, and a fire glows with the possibility of shelter and comfort at the end of a long journey. Hospitality is embedded in the idea of the hearth, and fire's romantic association with our past selves and historical cultures are not soon forgotten. While the fire itself is simply a source of warmth and light, its actual atmospheric importance far outweighs its practical usage.

Create a central focal point of the room wherein everyone can gather around comfortably (the basic idea of a hearth) such as a low coffee table surrounded by cushions and blankets to sit on, or a scattering of comfy chairs that are set up to invite conversation. Most of us automatically make our television set/entertainment center the focal point of our living area; while there is nothing inherently wrong with this, it isn't the best way to set up a space for interaction and togetherness. If that's how your living area is arranged, consider setting up a secondary hearth area for those hyggelige times, such as when the electronics are silent, and the guests are interacting.

Bedrooms

Obviously, guest bedrooms should be as warm and inviting as your own. In fact, many home experts will suggest you spend a night or two in your own guest bedroom to see what creature comforts are missing before subjecting your friends or family to it! Clearly, the beds should be warm with plenty of blankets, and everything should be tidy with space enough to accommodate guests.

Some other small things to think about that can make all the difference in a hygge home: have some books available for anyone to read, choosing topics with comfort and security in mind, as well as age appropriateness. Put out a small bowl or dish with non-perishable snacks in them so that a guest can help herself to a midnight snack if she likes. Decorate with some fairy lights if candles aren't a feasible option. Put out a couple of personal keepsakes as decoration, rather than something without emotional charge. Again, think of what you want to have at hand when you spend quality time in your bedroom during an afternoon or overnight. Your guest should want to stay in bed an extra hour or two, just for the sheer pleasure or relaxation.

Bathrooms

One of the undeniable facts about bathrooms is that they tend to accumulate clutter quickly. They contain items we use every day, and it becomes the path of least resistance to leaving everything lying about. In a hygge home, you should consider two things to complement the whole home atmosphere you've worked hard to set up. First, find a reasonable place to put away everything that you use daily, and then – if you don't have a space for everything, *consider minimizing your bathroom clutter*. Since one of the points of hygge is appreciating simplicity, perhaps you don't need four different kinds of shampoo, or ten different shades of eye shadow. This is part of the mindset of living a simple, present life.

In terms of a guest bathroom, think comfort: warm, soft towels with extras just in case, a drawer or cabinet with common toiletry items for guests to use when needed, some bath products and comfy robes to encourage a soothing soak. Think of your bathroom as a minimalist spa area - you get the idea.

Kitchen and Dining

Besides the living area, the kitchen area is the most central part of the home, where you bring people together, providing nourishment and love. In addition to simple, hearty food, always have some warming drinks on hand, coffee and tea and cocoa for sure. Kitchen lighting can often be harsh - strong lighting is necessary for accurate cooking – so be sure to consider other light sources for when everyone gathers in the kitchen. Set out bowls of fruit as décor and/or a snack and be sure to keep the kitchen tidy like the rest of the house - it's impossible to cook well in a disorganized kitchen.

When dining, set the table. It doesn't matter if your placemats, tablecloths, dishes, or glasses are expensive and fancy; it matters that you are creating an atmosphere. Paper plates and plastic cups just don't scream warm and inviting, and self-service at the table is far more attractive and interactive than grabbing a plate and loading it up yourself before wandering into the living room to eat in front of the television. Two rules of thumb in my own household is that dinner is never eaten with the television on or devices in hand, and the table is always set - however humbly - with individual place settings and platters and bowls set out for everyone to help themselves family style. For many, this may sound like extra work, but if you practice hygge with the right spirit, it is another way to build community and relationships around the table, as well as encouraging everyone to contribute.

Outside the Home

Even though this next depends in part on where you live, creating a hygge home also entails having an outdoor space for gathering and interacting. This can be a back porch with a comfortable set of chairs arranged around a portable hearth or firepit. It can be a balcony with some lovely plants and a view. It could be a garden equipped with a gazebo or a central picnic area. It could even be a driveway, some foldout chairs, and a good sunset. Whatever your situation, the hygge home should have some sort of outdoor component, weather permitting. An improvised picnic in the backyard is just as hyggelige as warming your hands around a campfire.

The Checklist

✓ The atmosphere is everything, and lighting is perhaps the most crucial aspect of creating the right hygge atmosphere. Candles are key, but there are many other ways to provide soft, natural-looking light, as well.

✓ Keep it pure and simple: hygge is about minimalist comfort, not clutter and consumption.

✓ Think about a hearth, whether it be a roaring fire, a virtual one, or an improvised focal point to your living area. There should be a comfortable gathering place in which good conversation and good company are fostered.

✓ Décor should complement the hygge atmosphere rather than detract; think of found materials, natural elements, and neutral colors for the best results.

✓ Think of all five senses when creating your hygge home: sight (lighting, color scheme, tidiness), sound (soft music or natural noise), smell (baking bread, dried flowers, other natural scents), touch (soft blankets, natural textures), and taste (warming drinks, simple and hearty food, sweet snacks).

✓ Think of every room in your house as a sanctuary of sorts, a calm and comforting refuge that encourages both independent self-care and communal togetherness.

Chapter 5: Practical Hygge: How to Hygge Your Wardrobe

Hygge is not just for your home or your holiday, it is also for your everyday living. According to some of the foremost experts on hygge (namely, Meik Wiking, as mentioned in Chapter 1), just about everything you do and own can be "hygge'd." Thus, fashion trends have also caught up with the explosion of popularity regarding this Danish lifestyle, and if you want to look - and feel - the part, designers and outlets have more than enough to offer. Likewise, making your wardrobe more hygge in spirit need not cost a fortune, as the keyword is comfort - you probably have some hyggelige items in your closet right now.

Keeping in line with all the aforementioned information regarding hygge style, your hygge'd wardrobe would consist of neutral colors, some insist on lots of black, and soft textures, with scarfs and cozy socks galore. The layering of clothes is also in the hygge spirit, and this makes sense as the trend is coming from a chilly winter climate.

Why hygge your wardrobe? To help yourself feel an overall sense of well-being, to feel that your lifestyle is embracing you in a warming hug, you need to feel warm and comfortable in all your clothes. Learning to relax and stay in the present moment during your daily life requires clothes that aren't fussy, that can be stylish without being uncomfortable, that can be minimalist yet fashion-forward. As with any wardrobe, there are excellent hygge styles for the range of what you do, from going out to a café to biking or cavorting in the park to staying in for dinner with the family. Anything in the hygge style will be relaxed and comfortable, and the fact that the fashion world has caught wind of this trend means that some of it can be quite beautiful in an understated manner.

Basically, you want your clothing to match your mood. Just as your home décor sets an atmosphere conducive to the stress-free happiness of hygge, so can your wardrobe set the stage for a feeling of hygge that goes with you everywhere.

The Checklist

✓ Knitwear is essential to the hygge style. Not only is it comfortable and affordable, but it is also easy to take care of - no special care instructions, for the most part. Soft and flowing lines define the style.

✓ Oversize separates are also very much in keeping with the trend of hygge, especially oversize sweaters. This is a style that never really goes out of fashion, in any case - at least around the house. For going out, a neutrally colored cardigan is the perfect accessory to round out an outfit *and* to keep you warm throughout the day.

✓ Socks, socks, and more socks: one of the primary components of any hygge wardrobe is an ample supply of cozy, comfy socks - bulky for wearing around the house, especially when you're curled up in your hyggekrog reading a book, and sleeker socks for treks to the café to fit into your favorite pair of loafers.

✓ Athletic leisurewear has dominated the fashion industry for years now; the hygge twist on that is fleece wear. A bit looser and softer, fleece pants free you from the stiffness of denim and can be dressed up or down, depending on the occasion. Try a comfortable blazer to dress them up or stick to an oversized sweater or cardigan for more casual wear.

✓ Aside from comfy socks, the most signature hygge fashion item is the scarf. Like the oversized sweater, the scarf comes in an almost endless variety of shapes and sizes, from big and bulky a la Harry Potter, or sleek and skinny. Whatever your preference, keep in mind that the scarf is not only a fashion accessory but a necessary piece of clothing in colder climates: scarfs should be both practical and pretty to fit the hygge spirit.

✓ Also, don't ditch the sweater - or even the scarf - during the warmer months of spring or early fall. Instead, look for less bulky and/or less lengthy sweaters and sleek scarfs of lightweight material to accentuate your look any time of the year. The function of these is to give you a feeling of comfortable security, even if you don't need absolutely need them for the practical purpose of warmth.

✓ Layering your look is also very hyggelige. Like the oversized sweater and the bulky scarf, layering can serve a very practical purpose and is also in keeping with the free spirit that underlies the hygge philosophy. In addition, this is another nod to the actual climate out of which hygge grows: the weather in Denmark is notoriously changeable, so layering is an excellent way to be prepared for whatever the weather happens to throw your way. It may be gloomy on your way to the office, but sunny and warmer by the time you bike over to meet your friends at the local café, or vice versa. As one famous Danish saying goes, "In Denmark, there is no bad weather, only bad clothes." Layering prepares you for any kind of weather and allows you to enjoy your day - no matter what the heavens dictate.

✓ Robes for wear around the house are absolutely hyggelige, as well. Keeping a robe handy for whatever season is an excellent way to invite self-care and moderate indulgence. Stepping into a comfy robe out of the shower in the morning practically begs you to brew another mug of coffee or cocoa and sit in your cozy nook with a book or a crafting project. Invest in at least a couple, one for warmer months and one for colder.

✓ As mentioned above, neutral colors are more in tune with the hygge spirit than bold or bright colors and patterns. Pale hues like beiges and whites are certainly hygge, though black is another popular choice. Muted black -like charcoal - are very much a part of hygge fashion. Wearing all black - especially in slightly varying shades - is quite chic without being severe if it's done with hygge in mind (that is, loose, flowing, and layered).

✓ An actual Danish fashion import is also a must-have for fashionable acolytes of hygge: the style of the sweater worn by Sarah Lund, the main character in the immensely popular television series, *The Killing*. It can be described as an ever-so-slightly oversized knit sweater with a bit of an understated pattern on it. This is the perfect sweater for an afternoon outing during cooler months.

✓ Remember: even if you are going out for a more formal evening, it is possible to capture the spirit of hygge: stay warm, above all else. Don't be afraid to layer a long comfortable cardigan or woolen jacket with a fancy dress for eveningwear. If there's one thing hygge doesn't support, it's feeling cold - quite the opposite of well-being or the warmth of a hug.

✓ In terms of your hygge wardrobe, it is primarily, a wardrobe centered around the same feeling of staying in a cozy, warm, and comfortable house. Thus, most of your hygge wardrobe doesn't have to be fancy or new or impressive. If you were to think in highly fashionable terms, you could think about coordinating your wardrobe with your interior design - both practical and in keeping with the hygge spirit. Either way, you undoubtedly have a handful of comfortable sweaters, cardigans, and fleece pants for your everyday home wear already; utilize those and invest in a few nicer items for meeting friends or going out to dinner. Now you have a personal hygge style to take with you anywhere!

✓ You can also think about hygge beyond your wardrobe into your beauty regimen itself. The hygge style is pure and simple, and this is exactly what your skincare and makeup regime should also be. A neutral color palette, excellent moisturizers, and maybe some essential oils and exfoliant are all you need to maintain a lovely glow that comes from both within – practicing the happiness of hygge – and from without.

In the spirit of hygge, celebrate the little joys in life and stay present in every moment: this shouldn't require you to overthink your daily attire, or to feel obligated to dress for someone else's ideals. Self-care means respecting the self, just as you take the time to nurture your physical health. In this way, a hygge wardrobe celebrates a woman's desire to look pretty without submitting herself to the whims of the others: other women, men, or fashion magazines. This does not mean that dressing in hygge style is not attractive or sexy! Hygge dress attire is simply designed by women for a woman's needs. It's pretty and practical, comfortable and cozy - an excellent way to present yourself as a working woman, as a woman of means, as a mother, as a friend. It should express your personal style and savvy.

A hygge mindset is also about slowing down and reducing excess. Your wardrobe can – and should – express that; coordinating an inordinate number of fussy accessories isn't in the spirit of enjoying your daily life without encumbrance. Practical considerations should drive the choice of accessories rather than any top-down kind of fashionista thinking. This puts you in the driver's seat, prompting you to become an active consumer rather than a passive purchaser. Again, practical can be pretty - sometimes even prettier than artifice. So, when considering your hygge lifestyle, remember to let your natural beauty shine through – even through your choice of attire.

Hygge is also about relaxation, avoiding the daily grind that often drives people to succumb to pressures and external demands rather than internal joys and practical pleasures. It is difficult to feel relaxed in clothing that is restrictive or *so bright and bold* that all eyes are on you all the time. Instead of working so diligently to impress others, we should be working hard to help ourselves to happiness and serenity. One way to turn down the pressures of everyday life is to allow yourself to wear clothing that is comfortable and free, that reminds you of how to maintain a sense of calm security.

Ultimately, hygge - especially for working women, torn between so many conflicting demands - is about being kinder to yourself. Giving yourself the time, space, and permission to relax and to enjoy the simple pleasures in life is one of the greatest gifts you can give yourself. In this current era of constant self-improvement, we are told that we must work harder and harder to get healthier and better. This fallacy often reads as one simple thing, especially for women: thinner. While there is a contemporary rage for all things authentic (from food to craft beer to old-world artisanal products to repurposed furniture and handmade pickles), this new vogue tends to skip over women in terms of how they are asked to present themselves. Supermodels and movie stars dominate the pages of glossy magazines, movie screens, and our televisions; for most, this idea of beauty is both unattainable and unhealthy. This is where the influence of hygge is slowly-but-surely being felt. Over the past couple of decades, changes in social attitudes, and the rapid growth of technology have allowed us to see many kinds of people in all shapes, sizes, and profiles of beauty. Hygge is one trend that has embraced the idea that beauty isn't simply one ideal, and it shouldn't be difficult or uncomfortable. Indeed, it should be easy, cozy, comfortable, and uniquely *you*. This philosophy has been a driving force behind Danish culture for many years, and it has led to one of the most female-friendly cultures in the world - not to mention giving birth to the happiest people on earth! Hygge is not merely a passing trend, but a true way of life that could teach us all a little about self-love and kindness.

Chapter 6: Practical Hygge: Hungry for Hygge

As with any long-standing tradition in any culture across the world, food plays a significant role. It would be difficult to think of Thanksgiving without turkey, for example, or to imagine St. Patrick's Day without soda bread and beer. Aside from these secular examples, cultures with deep-seated religious traditions also have accompanying foods, such as matzo during Passover or dates to break the daily fast during Ramadan. Denmark is overwhelmingly Christian in its religious traditions, and we will discuss how hygge and holidays - Christmas and Easter, for example - work together in the next chapter. Hygge itself is an entrenched secular tradition in Danish culture, and it also gives rise to particular kinds of foods and drinks that have a specific spirit of well-being and comfort.

What makes a food hyggelige? Warm and welcoming comfort foods fit the category to a tee: just as the word hygge can be etymologically traced back to "hug," the foods you eat while practicing hygge should represent a hug from the inside-out. Since hygge is also about communion between family and friends, hyggelige food is meant to be shared with loved ones at the table –

with plenty of conversation and interaction. This can be in a café, having some fika (snacks to be consumed with warm drinks), or it can be in your own home, enjoying a home-cooked dinner. Hygge isn't directly concerned with health - a sugar bun is very hygge while celery sticks are decidedly not - but it does encourage moderation. The hygge emphasis on outdoor activity certainly balances the significant cocoa and cake consumption, or at least that is the idea! Eating hyggelige isn't about guilt or self-restraint; it is about health in the sense of self-care, comfort, and communion with others. Breaking bread with others has always been a sacrosanct act, and hygge emphasizes the joys and pleasures of sharing food around a crowded table.

Buns and Bread for Breakfast

As hearsay would have it, breakfast is the most important meal of the day, and that couldn't be truer when starting your hyggelige day. A large, steaming mug of coffee or cocoa (or tea, if one prefers) is a must to get you going on a chilly morning, accompanied by a hearty breakfast to fuel you on your bike ride, for your daily work, or simply to encourage you to get a fire going before you settle into your cozy nook with a good book. The following recipes are just a quick representation of all that Danish food has to offer for breaking the fast each morning. Remember: hygge food doesn't have to be exclusively Danish! A freshly baked biscuit with some sausage gravy or a plate of warm waffles stuffed with either pecans or bacon and covered in syrup would also fit the bill quite nicely. Try these ideas below for a more specifically Scandinavian approach to the first meal of the day.

Note: all the recipes in this chapter are rendered as a set of instructions, more method than the recipe in the traditional parlance of cookbooks. Read through each step carefully before gathering ingredients and beginning to cook.

Rugbrød: Danish Rye Bread

Makes two loaves

This traditional recipe seems a bit intimidating at first, but once you get past the list of ingredients and become accustomed to making a sourdough starter, this is a delicious and hearty bread for any time of the day.

    o Stir together with a scant cup each of cracked rye kernels, cracked wheat, flax seeds, and sunflower seeds. To that, add 1 ½ cups of sourdough starter (there are many simple ways to make this, using just yeast, flour, and water - the internet has a variety of recipes), 3 cups of water, and 1-2 tablespoons of malted syrup (molasses will do in a pinch). Combine all these ingredients in the evening before you plan to bake your loaves, letting everything soak for about 8 hours or so.

    o The next morning, add 1 ½ cups each of rye flour and all-purpose flour, along with 1 tablespoon of salt. Let the dough rise for about 1-½ hours.

    o Bake the loaves in two standard loaf pans in a pre-heated oven at 350 degrees for about an hour. Take your loves from the loaf pans, allowing them to cool a bit before slicing and slathering with butter or salted/sweetened yogurt or jam.

Porridge: Staple Food

Though many things could be named the national dish of Denmark, porridge would most certainly be in the running. There are as many recipes for porridge as there are Danes themselves! Here is one simple take on this classic staple, quite above and beyond the microwave oatmeal of American childhood.

    o For *one serving*, stir together about 4 ½ ounces of oatmeal (or other hearty grain, such as farro, spelt, or quinoa - cooking times will vary, of course) with a cup of water in a small saucepan. Add a cored and diced apple and ½ cup of berries (blueberries, blackberries, raspberries), along with 1/3 cup of chopped nuts, almond, pecans, or walnuts work well. Throw in a pinch or two of salt and let simmer until thickened and grains are tender. Once off the heat, serve with a few splashes of milk or cream - or a dollop of yogurt - and add a touch more salt for a savory take. You might add a little honey for sweetness.

As you can see, this recipe is most definitely a basic method to build according to your own tastes and what happens to be in your pantry or fridge. In keeping with the tradition of frugality, the Danes also like to make porridge out of stale rugbrød, with raisins, dried citrus peel, honey, and warming spices.

Ebleskivers: Danish Pancakes

Makes about three dozen

These fluffy pancake-like creations could be served for afternoon tea - or fika, as it is commonly called in Denmark - as well as breakfast. While there is a special ebleskiver pan to encourage these cakes to retain a biscuit-like shape and help them rise, you can easily cook them in a skillet or on a griddle like traditional American-style pancakes.

> o Whisk together 2 cups of flour, a teaspoon each of baking powder and baking soda, a generous pinch of salt, and a ¼ teaspoon of cinnamon in a large mixing bowl. Set this aside while you prepare the wet ingredients.
> o In another mixing bowl, beat 3 egg whites until they form stiff peaks - this will help the ebleskivers rise and contribute to their lightness.
> o In another bowl, beat the 3 egg yolks with a couple of tablespoons of sugar until incorporated, and then slowly beat in 2 cups of buttermilk and 2 teaspoons of vanilla. Mix in your dry ingredients, and then gently fold in your beaten egg whites.
> o For each small pancake, use a rounded tablespoon of batter. To each, add a teaspoon of finely diced fruit - peeled

apples are the most traditional, but you can also use peaches, pears, or even small berries. Cook on a well-oiled griddle, skillet, or in an ebleskiver pan until the edges start to bubble and bottoms begin to lightly brown. Flip and cook for a minute more, then serve dusted with powdered sugar or topped with a dollop of whipped cream.

Lunch and Lighter Fare

Lunch is usually a lighter affair in Denmark, coming as it does between the two cherished traditions of a hearty, warming breakfast and the afternoon delights of the café for fika (coffee and a sweet snack). The recipes below provide just a quick sample of what might be on the menu, but there are innumerable variations on these themes. The category of smørrebrød itself is merely a blank canvas for any number of ingredients, and the popularity of soup provides a dizzying array of options, from pumpkin/squash to cauliflower to split pea – the list goes on! In addition, lunch might also be a hearty vegetable casserole or a savory variation on porridge. Lots of popular American fare could be considered a very hygge lunch: macaroni and cheese, for example, or a big bowl of pasta with ragu or pesto, or the ever-popular chicken pot pie; these are all warming, simple-yet- delicious meals that are very much in keeping with the spirit of hygge.

Smørrebrød: Infinite Variety

Smørrebrød essentially refers to an open-faced sandwich, usually eaten with knife and fork, topped with a nearly infinite variety of meats, cheeses, vegetables, and so on. These lunchtime treats are inescapably linked to Scandinavian countries, where they are a symbol of the simplicity and conviviality of the various peoples who reside there. Start with a decently thick slab of good bread – your choice, though rye is traditional for most smørrebrød – then slather with some rich butter, topping it all with favored ingredients. Some combinations you might enjoy trying:

- Cold-smoked salmon with thinly sliced cucumber and lots of chopped, fresh dill
- Sliced hard-boiled egg with avocado spears and thinly sliced radishes
- Pickled herring or liver pâté with thinly sliced red onion and chopped parsley
- Some good Havarti cheese with sliced tomato and chopped chives
- Cured meats, such as salami or ham, with onions, tomatoes, and/or herbs

In short, just about anything you have in your fridge and/or garden would work in these open-faced sandwiches. Just don't forget the smear of butter and the heartiness of toppings. After all, these are knife-and-fork affairs.

Tomato Soup, Nordic Style

8-10 servings

Most - and I mean 99.99 percent - of American kids have enjoyed the lunchtime staple of hot tomato soup with grilled cheese. It's a classic, whether made from a can of Campbell's soup with Wonder Bread and a plastic-wrapped slice of cheese, or from some roasted garden tomatoes with local sourdough bread wrapped around artisanal cheddar. It's also very, very hygge: warm, comforting, familiar, simple, and delightfully delicious. The following recipe is a more Danish style take on that classic combo.

- Chop 1 onion, 2 or 3 cloves of garlic, a scant half pound of celeriac (celery root), and a couple of carrots, then sauté together in a large pot in 3 tablespoons olive oil until everything is softened a bit.
- Add 3 cups of chopped tomatoes (canned will work just fine), 2 tablespoons of tomato paste, 1 cup wine (usually a dry white, but you can experiment), and about 8 cups of stock. Homemade stock is always best, of course, but whatever you have the time for; remember that this is hygge

cooking and we are not supposed to be stressing about it! For a more traditional or vegan version, consider using vegetable or mushroom stock.

o Simmer everything together until all vegetables are cooked through and tender and the soup thickens slightly about ten or fifteen minutes. Serve either with cooked rye berries stirred in, or with a couple of thick slices of rugbrød, slathered with butter or topped with Edam cheese and broiled.

Hot Smoked Salmon: Scandinavian Staple

Serves 4

Salmon, along with herring, are also clear markers of Scandinavian food, ubiquitous throughout the region. Cold smoked salmon is best left to the experts unless you have the specialized equipment, but hot smoked salmon can be easily made in a home kitchen. Pair this with a nice green salad, and you have a satisfying meal.

o Make a cure for one pound of salmon. You can use any kind of fish, like a firm, fatty fish such as like steelhead trout, but skin-on sockeye is perhaps most popular. Combine 2 cups of brown sugar with 1 cup kosher salt, 1 tablespoon of freshly ground black pepper, and a teaspoon each of ground coriander seed and juniper berries. *Optional: add grated zest from a couple of oranges for bright sweetness.* Let cure in the refrigerator for a couple of hours.

o Set up your smoker. There are inexpensive, commercially available stovetop smokers which are very easy to use, and these are worth the small investment if you think you'll do this more than a couple of times a year. They are also great for smoking shellfish, tomatoes, and other vegetables, as well as small pieces of meat. If you don't have one, then create a makeshift smoker using a heavy pan with a lid, some aluminum foil, and some wood chips or dried tea leaves. To do this, put a layer of aluminum foil in your pan then scatter your wood chips over this layer. You can use tea and whole spices with the chips or instead of the chips; either way imparts flavor to your meat/fish. On top of the chips or spices, put down another layer of tin foil. Put your salmon into a steamer basket or tray, lower into the smoker, and cover with the lid. Turn your stove's heat to high and watch, with lid ajar, until you see wisps of smoke coming from the pan. Cover tightly, turn heat to medium so as not to burn your chips too quickly. Smoked your salmon for about 40 minutes until it flakes easily with a fork. If you like, baste a few times with some maple syrup for a lacquered look and a sweeter taste.

Café: Living the Fika Life

The importance of café culture to Denmark and other Scandinavian countries cannot be overstated; fika describes a daily ritual to take an afternoon break and meet with friends for coffee or cocoa and a quick snack. Cakes of all kinds are very common, as are various pastries and other sugary delicacies. As with many Danish foods, there is often a healthy dose of warming spices, such as cinnamon and cardamom, to be found in many traditional desserts. It is worth noting that many of the cakes, puddings, and pastries featured in cafes are also served for dessert - and breakfast.

Sugar Buns: Nearly No Effort Cinnamon Buns

Makes 12

Essentially, the following is a tasty recipe that has been hygge-fied into simplicity. Traditional cinnamon rolls take yeast and rising time and more complicated baking methods. These sugar buns can be made with easily purchased ingredients in the space of about half an hour. These are so easy and versatile that you'll likely have them on hand regularly once you try them.

    o Make some cinnamon sugar: combine 2 tablespoons each of granulated sugar and dark brown sugar (pack it tightly when measuring), a teaspoon of cinnamon, and a pinch of salt. Set aside while you prepare the dough.

o Sprinkle a tablespoon of granulated sugar onto a work surface, then unfold one sheet of already prepared and thawed - but still cold - puff pastry over this. Thaw in the refrigerator overnight for best results. You can also use an equal amount of other purchased doughs, such as crescent roll or biscuit dough (2 cans worth) or a pound of pizza dough. Spread 2 tablespoons of softened butter over dough, then sprinkle with a third of your cinnamon-sugar mixture; pat lightly or press lightly with a rolling pin to be sure that sugar sticks to dough, then roll up tightly, starting with long end. Cut into 6 equal portions. Repeat with remaining dough, saving the last third of cinnamon sugar for sprinkling on top.

o Place portions cut side up into buttered muffin tin wells, and then bake at 400 degrees for 20-25 minutes, until puffed and lightly browned. Melt another 4 tablespoons of butter, brush over the top of baked buns, and then sprinkle with reserved cinnamon sugar. Unmold from the pans while they are still warm.

Risalamande: Danish Rice Pudding

Serves Six

Rice pudding is a beloved dessert the world over, and the Danish do it especially well. Risalamande is traditionally served as a dessert at Christmas; however, a simpler version of it is eaten year-round. The Christmas version is dressed up with a cherry sauce if you'd like to splurge, but the basic recipe is just as tasty for an everyday treat.

o Bring 1-¼ cups of water to a boil, then add 1-2/3 cups of short grain rice, and let boil for a couple of minutes. Stir in a split vanilla bean pod and 7 cups of whole milk; bring back to a boil, then cover and lower heat, simmering for 15 to 20 minutes, stirring occasionally, until rice is just past al dente stage. Remove from heat and discard the vanilla pod.

o Transfer cooked rice to a bowl, and stir in 2 tablespoons granulated sugar, a teaspoon of salt, and the scraped seeds from another vanilla bean pod. Whip 2 cups heavy cream until soft peaks form, then fold gently into rice pudding, in three batches. Add 1-¼ cups chopped blanched almonds. At Christmas time, it is traditional to hide a whole blanched almond in the pudding, where some lucky diner will find it and be granted good fortune throughout the year. Taste for sweetness, correct if necessary, and then chill.

o For extra decadence and a beautiful presentation, make a cherry sauce for topping! Start by simmering 1-½ pounds of pitted cherries (you can use frozen for ease) with ¾ cup of granulated sugar, another split vanilla bean pod, and 2 cups of water. Simmer for about 15 minutes, then mix 3 tablespoons of cornstarch with 2 tablespoons of water and stir this slurry into your cherry mixture. Cook until it thickens nicely, about 5 more minutes. Taste to see if it's sweet enough for your liking. Serve the cold pudding topped with hot cherry sauce for a lovely contrast in flavors, textures, and temperatures.

Sticky Chocolate Cake: Because Everyone Needs Chocolate

Serves six to eight people

A Scandinavian version of what we call - though a misnomer – "flourless chocolate cake" or "lava cake," this is a satisfyingly decadent dessert treat - and still quite simple - that just begs a cup of coffee to go with it.

o Combine ½ cup flour with ¼ cup cocoa powder and a generous pinch of salt. Beat two eggs with 1-¼ cups of granulated sugar, then add dry mixture. Drizzle in ½ cup of melted butter and 1 tablespoon of vanilla, then pour into a greased 8-inch pie pan.

o Back in the lower rack of a 300-degree oven for about half an hour. The center should be slightly set; it may take an additional five minutes or so, depending on the accuracy of your oven. Let the cake set up for an hour in the pan, then serve while still slightly warm or refrigerate for a fudgy treat the next day. This is probably not complete without some freshly whipped cream (or a scoop of ice cream) and some fresh berries.

Dinner: Slow-Cooked and Homemade

One of the attributes of hygge is to slow down and take your time to be present in your daily life, enjoying the little things as they come your way. Dinnertime is the perfect chance to take it low and slow, making a dinner that is both nutritious and indulgent, satisfying and hearty. A quick trip to the market and a few hours of patient waiting - during which you are engaging in activities with your kids, conversation with your friends, or wrapped up by the hearth reading a book - fill the home with wonderful and comforting smells, followed by a delicious dinner with family and friends. There are many traditional dinner foods that are classic hygge treats, such as the famed Swedish meatballs (made all over Scandinavia) or warming stews and big bowls of dumplings. There are any number of classic multicultural favorites in American cuisine that would easily qualify as hygge, from Italian lasagna or spaghetti and meatballs to Irish beef stew and soda bread to Chinese hotpot or Middle Eastern mezze to typical Midwestern casserole dishes, like Minnesota's famed hot dish. Basically, for a dinner to be hygge, it must be hearty and wholesome, simple and satisfying, not overly complicated or time-consuming, giving everyone time for togetherness and fellowship.

Braised Short Ribs: Timeless Classic

Serves 4-6

Just about every culture has some version of a long-cooked braise, and these short ribs are found all over countries with cold climes and cattle. The preparation time is reasonable, and the rest is merely patience and sides. These can be served on a bed of mashed potatoes, or better yet, mashed potatoes spiked with celeriac (celery root), mashed or roasted rutabagas or another turnip, or over a bed of buttered noodles. Add a quick green salad, and you have a full meal.

○ The very simplest version of this is to make a mirepoix of two diced onions, three carrots, and three stalks of celery, sautéed in olive oil for a few minutes. Add roughly six pounds of bone-in beef short ribs, a couple of bay leaves, and a bottle of red wine or 4 cups stock or water (or a combination to equal 4-5 cups), then cover and cook in a 325 degree oven for 3 or 4 hours, until the ribs are fall off the bone tender. But there are several variations and/or additions that will add flavor and sophistication to the dish:

○ Brown your short ribs on all sides before you add the mirepoix, scraping up the browned bits on the bottom of the pan, which add layers of flavor. Brown ribs in batches so that you avoid steaming them, then sauté mirepoix before returning ribs to pot (a Dutch oven is best).

○ Soak an ounce of dried mushrooms in hot water for half an hour, then chop and add to mirepoix for heightened umami (savory depth) of flavor.

○ Speaking of umami, for another boost you can add a tablespoon of anchovy paste, soy sauce, or fish sauce along with mirepoix.

○ Add some sprigs of fresh rosemary or other appropriate dried herbs (oregano, thyme, winter savory) and some chopped garlic for extra flavor notes.

○ As with many braises, this is often even better the next day; letting the braise rest overnight in the refrigerator also gives you control over how fatty and flavorful the sauce is. After the braise is cooled, refrigerate overnight, then skim off hardened fat, and separate meat from liquid (you can shred the meat at this point, if you like, depending on how you will serve it). Strain liquid and adjust seasonings or add the slurry to thicken it to pour over the finished dish.

Hasselback Potatoes: Vegetarian Delight

Serves 4

Having a hygge meal doesn't always preclude vegetarians. While Denmark is certainly a meat-eating country (as most northern European countries are), it is certainly forward-thinking in terms of health and can be vegetarian-friendly. These lovely potatoes, versions of which are served all over Scandinavia, are one such dish that is hearty enough to be a main, served alongside a green salad, and perhaps some roasted sprouts or braised cabbage.

> o Basically, these are baked potatoes that are fanned out in order to create a more browned interior and slightly more interesting texture and look than a regular baked potato. Take four large baking potatoes and cut small horizontal slits in them along the length of the potato; the idea is to leave the potato whole, so don't cut all the way through to the bottom. The best way to do this is to position the potato between two wooden-handled spoons (or chopsticks), then to cut until the knife hits the barrier. You want the cuts to be as close as possible, about ¼ to 1/8 of an inch apart. Wrap prepped potatoes in foil, then bake in a 400-degree oven for about 40 minutes (depending on the size of the potato, this may take longer). Unwrap the potatoes and brush all over and in between slits with olive oil (vegan version) or melted butter, and season well with salt and pepper. Return to oven, unwrapped, and bake for an additional 15 or 20 minutes.
>
> o If you'd like to fancy these up a bit - a nice idea (especially if they are to be the main course) is to then add some slices of cheese. Gruyere would be fantastic here, or crumbles of blue cheese placed between the slits. Then return the potatoes to the oven briefly, allowing your cheese slices t to melt. To keep it vegan, add some chopped fresh chives, parsley, and

garlic to add some oomph. Use your imagination, as well, if you're not restrained by dietary needs: you could stuff the slits with thinly sliced ham and Swiss cheese, or in a nod to Jansson's temptation, some chopped anchovies.

Pork and Christmas Cabbage: Special Occasion

6 servings

Flaeskesteg is a popular and festive dish at Christmas, and while it is still quite simple to prepare, it does take some planning to track down a good piece of pork with the skin still attached. Christmas cabbage is a brilliantly hued dish of pickled red cabbage that is traditionally served on Christmas Eve. The wonderful thing about both recipes is that they are so truly simple while being very special.

> o The hardest part about the pork dish is finding a nice pork roast with the skin on; you may have to special order this if you don't live near a good butcher or a well-stocked market. In any case, you'll want a 5-7-pound pork roast with skin on. Score the skin all over, being careful not to cut into the meat below. Put the pork on a rack in a roasting pan that has been stocked with a quartered onion or two, some sprigs of rosemary and/or thyme, and a cup of water. The drippings from the pork will combine with the aromatics below to create the base for a simple sauce if you like. Rub the pork all over with butter and season generously with salt.
> o Roast the pork for about two hours at 400 degrees, making sure that the liquid in the roasting pan never quite runs out. When the roast is done, strain the drippings and skim off the fat; reserve to make the sauce. Before serving, return the roast to the oven under the broiler for a few minutes, to crisp up the skin - be careful not to let this burn.
> o Meanwhile, make the sauce: boil the strained skimmed drippings for a few minutes until slightly thickened. Add a couple of splashes of cream to this with salt and pepper to

taste. For added flavor, crumble is some blue cheese or add a couple of tablespoons of tart jelly, such as red currant.

o For the Christmas cabbage, simmer a shredded head of red cabbage, 2 cups each granulated sugar and white vinegar, 3 cups of water, and 2 teaspoons of salt in a large pot for about an hour. Leftovers are excellent, served cold on a sandwich.

Warming Drinks

Finally, any day that is filled with the hygge spirit will also include some warming drinks, no matter the time of year. Certainly, wintertime sees more cocoa made and spiced (and spiked) drinks abound, but coffee is ubiquitous throughout the year in Danish homes and cafes, and tea is also gaining a foothold in this more globalized climate. No breakfast or trip to the café would be complete without a warming drink. Expand your repertoire with the following recipes.

Hot and Spicy Cocoa

Serves 12 (or 6 twice, if you're having a really hygge day)

o For the hot chocolate mix, combine a cup each of unsweetened cocoa powder and granulated sugar, a tablespoon of cinnamon, and ½ teaspoon each of ground ginger and nutmeg (freshly grated is great, but whatever you have on hand will do). For extra flavor, add a pinch or two of ground cardamom and, for more spice, add ½ teaspoon of ground chipotle powder. For each serving, use 3 tablespoons of the mixture stirred into 1 ½ cups of hot milk, preferably whole milk.

o Another bonus: use vanilla sugar for some of your sugar mixes. This is easy to make from home with the spent pods of vanilla beans that you've used to make the rice pudding above. Just bury the pods in some sugar in a tightly sealed jar (thoroughly washed old mayonnaise or pickle jars are great for this). Shake every few days. After a couple of weeks, the sugar will be redolent of vanilla. Use in your coffee, too. Keep topping up with more sugar and spent pods as you go, making sure to distribute everything evenly, to keep a steady supply on hand.

Berry Merry Glögg

Serves 8-10

Mulled wines of all kinds are popular throughout the cold climates of Europe. This one is special because of the addition of berries and rum.

○ Simmer 4 cups of blackberries, blueberries, raspberries, or a combination thereof with ¼ to ½ cup of sugar, depending on how sweet you want the resulting drink to be, for about 10 minutes, until broken down and thickened. Puree with 3 cups of water in blender or food processor and push through a sieve.

○ Return the sieved puree to the pot and add your aromatics: zest from one orange (in a thick spiral), a couple of cinnamon sticks and star anise pods, some cardamom seeds, a split vanilla bean pod, and some cloves. Simmer this for 20 minutes or so, keeping the lid on to avoid excess evaporation. Add a bottle of red wine to this, along with some rum to taste; a generous splash is about right, but too little and it has no impact. Too much, and it overwhelms with alcohol. Heat this very gently so you don't boil off the alcohol, then ladle into mugs, leaving whole spices behind. Some people add raisins and blanched nuts to this, as well, for a warm drink and a snack all in one.

Mulled Cider

8 servings

○ This is made based on the same principles above, but it is simpler and can be either alcoholic or non-alcoholic.

○ Simmer two quarts of cider (again, alcoholic or not, depending on your desire) with a couple of cinnamon sticks, the zest of an orange, some cloves, and either cardamom pods or allspice berries. When warm and fragrant, serve in nice thick mugs.

Chapter 7: Practical Hygge: Hygge Holidays and Seasons

While hygge is most definitely associated with the Christmas holiday season and winter, it is certainly possible to practice hygge any time of the year. Indeed, as this philosophy becomes more popular across the globe, many people are applying hygge principles to holidays, festivals, and seasonal activities throughout the year. Of course, the Danes would suggest that this is quite right, as hygge is a mindset - not a passing mood. Any day is a good day for hygge, and throughout this chapter, you will find ideas for how to keep yourself engaged with the hygge spirit.

Winter: Hyggelige Season!

For too many of us, winter is a time to dread, with cold and blustery weather, complicated travel, holiday pressures, bored or sick kids stuck indoors at home. For the Danish people who embrace the philosophy of hygge, wintertime can be the most magical, comforting, coziest time of year. The essence of hygge truly embodies what we most love about wintertime: wrapping yourself in a blanket in front of a fire, wearing cozy socks, cooking comforting foods, and taking some time off your busy schedule for a little relaxing self-care and family celebration. No time of year is better suited for indulging in hygge. Some ideas for how to hygge up your winter follow below.

- o Since you can't spend too much time outside, bring nature inside: potted poinsettias are a holiday tradition that both brightens and soothes your home sanctuary.
- o If you do spend time outdoors, invest in (or make) a firepit; there's nothing more hygge than gathering around a roaring fire and roasting marshmallows with friends and family.
- o Also, don't forget about winter sports: if you're lucky enough to live where there's adequate snowfall, take the family out for sledding, skiing, or ice skating. These are excellent ways to bond as a family and make the best out of the colder weather while getting some healthy outdoor activity.
- o Consider a nighttime trek through the snow - with or without snowshoes, depending on your area – as there is nothing quite so magical as the glint of moonlight on freshly fallen snow.
- o If the cold eventually gets you down, take refuge in a café. You were going to anyway, right? That's a daily activity! Bump it up a notch, and instead of your regular haunt, visit a museum and take your afternoon fika in their café; most larger museums now have a small eating place on the grounds.
- o Create your own visual memories, taking out your camera to get some pictures of nature and family. Put together an album to share with everyone.
- o Don't forget about our fellow creatures - it's cold out there for everyone! Put out some food or a feeder for the birds and spend some hygge time watching and learning - an excellent way to involve kids in naturalist activities.
- o Think of your home bathroom like a spa retreat: invest in some bubble bath or bath salts, put on some relaxing music,

and have a warm and fluffy robe waiting for you at the end of a soothing bath.

o Remember that wintertime foods are not limited to holidays. There is no better time of year to indulge in a daily cup of cocoa than winter, breaking out the old fondue pot, and inviting your friends for a party. Be sure to have some mulled wine or cider on hand, as well.

o Tackle the stack of books on your nightstand: set up a hyggekrog (cozy nook) and indulge in some blissful hours of pleasurable reading. And, by the way, real books with some heft are far more hyggelige than reading on an electronic device. Just saying...

o Have a pajama day where the whole family stays in and lounges about, ideally indulging in both group activities. Board games, anyone? Movie marathon with popcorn and sweets? If not a group gathering, each can snuggle in with books.

o Start a treasure jar. Though this can be done at any time of the year, it's particularly potent during winter to see how nature changes from fall into spring. Collect small items from your daily walk or bike ride (you know, your hygge activity) and store them in a jar. At the end of the season, arrange and display your newfound treasures.

o Learn something new or teach something new - or both. Cook with your children, enroll in a class about something you've always wanted to learn, or teach yourself a different language.

o Do some stargazing - figuratively and literally. Make plans for the next season, drawing up your dream garden for the spring, thinking about your summer vacation, etc. Be sure not to forget to look up into the clear night sky and treasure the present (gratitude!) and dream of the future.

o

Christmas *Is* the Most Wonderful Hyggelige Time of the Year

In mainly Christian countries of the north, the holiday most associated with wintertime is Christmas. With this holiday comes a host of traditions that are very hyggelige - in fact, the very notion of upholding and creating tradition is part of the hygge spirit itself. Even if you celebrate another seasonal holiday (for example, Hanukkah or Kwanzaa), you can adapt some of these traditions for your own enjoyment.

o Lights, lights, and more lights! Fairy lights or twinkle lights can adorn every room in the house, along with candles and Christmas tree lights. Put them in clear jars or string them across bookshelves or wrap around railings.

o Write letters to Santa with your children. Encourage them to think of these letters not just as personal wish lists of material objects, but also of lists about what to be thankful for and what to look forward to in the new year.

o Decorate the house both inside and out with seasonal objects: reindeers and trees, elves and snowmen, lights and ornaments, wreaths and garlands. Make it a family activity and involve everyone in creating a special environment for a special time of year.

o Host a wrap party, either with family or friends (or both). Have everyone develop their own special skill, whether it be coordinating paper and ribbon, making bows, or using special lettering for gift cards.

o Make homemade gifts: jams and jellies, pickles and preserves, liqueurs and flavored libations are all welcome hostess gifts this time of year. If you have other skills, use these as well: sketch a drawing, paint a picture, or write and frame a poem. Pottery and woodworking crafts are also fabulous. These kinds of handmade gifts are truly priceless.

o Go and see a Christmas show with the family, whether it be local production of The Nutcracker or the latest

Christmas-themed movie. While you're at it, listen to some carols or take the family caroling around the neighborhood.

o Start a new tradition to return to each year: decorate personalized mugs for every member of the family; knit hats or scarves for friends, give dated ornaments to the special people in your life, host a marathon holiday movie weekend or have Christmas Eve brunch for neighbors and friends.

Spring: Renew and Re-energize

After the comforts (and challenges) of winter pass, many people look forward to the spring. It is naturally the time of year when our thoughts turn to renewal and rebirth; the birds start singing again, the earth awakens, and we return to the outdoors with renewed vigor. All these typical springtime feelings are completely compatible with the philosophy of hygge: working outdoors, playing outdoors, observing and respecting nature, feeling gratitude for the little miracles in our everyday lives, cozying up to a fulfilling project that allows us to spend time with family and friends. We may trade in our oversize sweaters for lighter cardigans and put the cozy socks and fire-building on hold for the moment, but there is nothing that says we must put our hygge mindset on pause. Some of the ways in which you can keep up your hyggelige practice are as follows:

o First and foremost, don't abandon your candles! There is nothing that says pretty in spring like small tea candles on a picnic table or in your dining room. Choose fresh but muted colors, like peach and pale green for an acknowledgment of the awakening natural scene outdoors. This lighting, along with opening your windows and letting fresh air and natural light in, will keep you in the hygge spirit every day.

o Flowers should also be a part of your hygge springtime. And, more importantly, these flowers should be natural flowers, found just outside your door - even the most humble-looking weed-like flower is beautiful in the right arrangement and under the right-minded gaze! Wildflowers in mason jars are evocative of springtime hygge in a surefire way.

o Play in the dirt! One of the most marvelous things about springtime is the opportunity to get outside and get your hand dirty: plant a garden, build a treehouse, or put in some more trees or hedgerows. Build something for the future in the glorious weather of spring.

o Speaking of the outdoors, be sure to go on a picnic or two, or ten, while the weather is perfect for such things. Fly a kite, play in the park, notice the ducklings hatching and the butterflies emerging. Introduce your children to the wonders of springtime rebirth.

o Speaking of the outdoors in inclement weather be sure to play in the rain! A gentle springtime rainfall is one of the most beautiful feelings in the world, especially to a young child in all his wonderment. And if you live in an area that gets some fierce spring weather - and that's most of us - enjoy it like you enjoy the wintertime. Marvel; at the power of nature while you are inside your safe haven with loved ones. These are the days built for hyggekrogs and reading binges.

o Look at your home décor and really think spring. Keep it minimalist and tidy, as hygge would have us do, but bring in a few lighter, somewhat brighter pieces to match the changing of the seasons outside. Put some fresh sheets on the bed and swap out your ultra-fuzzy robe for a sleek silk one to welcome in the warmer weather.

o As to cooking, springtime hygge is all about the market. Get yourself to the local farmers' market and indulge in all the rare and fleeting springtime treats such as fresh strawberries and asparagus, fava beans and sugar snap peas, baby lettuces and delicate herbs, spring chickens and their glorious eggs. There's a reason why Easter feasts typically feature devilled eggs and young lamb - it's just the right season for it. Check out some more Easter ideas below.

Easter Redux

Perhaps the ultimate celebration of renewal and rebirth is the hallowed holiday of Easter. No matter how you celebrate it, Easter is a lovely springtime opportunity to gather with family and friends around a table laden with food, sharing gratitude for all we are fortunate to have. Even if you don't celebrate Easter, there is ample opportunity to initiate a secular springtime festival, with some or all the ideas below:

○ Secret snowdrop letters: this is a Danish tradition at Easter, to send a crafted paper letter to a loved one, with a sweet and caring message, left unsigned. The tradition says that, if the recipient guesses that you sent the letter, you must give them an Easter egg; if they cannot guess who sent it, then they must give you an Easter egg. It's kind of like a Secret Santa for springtime. The trick is to cut out a beautiful paper design, as you might have done (depending on your age) in school with hearts for Valentine's Day or a paper daisy chain.

○ In terms of holiday décor, many Danes will even put up a kind of Easter tree with spring branches and other material from nature. It is adorned with symbols of fertility (like eggs) and rebirth (like feathers and flowers).

○ Speaking of eggs, certainly any Easter celebration is bereft without the traditional dyed eggs, of course, but to be extra-hygge about it, choose natural dyes that come from common kitchen items rather than chemical ones (for example: beet juice or chlorophyll extract). And, of course, you'll be doing this with children, family, and/or friends around your dining table.

○ Have an Easter egg hunt but try to make sure it's outside. Sometimes spring weather prohibits this, as people in my region well know! Every other year, it seems that Easter is freezing and forbidding outside. Nevertheless, if possible, gather for the hunt outside. If not outside, no worries! The idea of a playful task for children is hygge in and of itself.

o Don't forget to enjoy some special Easter treats, as well, the kinds of chocolate delights that come along only once a year - all the better if they are homemade, of course, but some purchased delicacies can become a yearly tradition, as well.

o Speaking of food, an Easter feast is always in order! Indeed, it can be one of the most indulgent of the year and the food itself is hyggelige in its very nature: fresh spring vegetables, a big comforting ham or leg of spring lamb, lush devilled eggs (to make use of all those handsomely dyed ones), braided Easter bread, and luscious desserts. Be sure to have a lovely centerpiece made with natural spring branches and other found materials. And candles! And lots of family and friends.

o Homemade Easter decorations are a treat and a way to practice hygge with your children and others. It is also very hyggelige to make gifts for your annual Easter baskets, whether they be edible or crafted - this shows how much you care for your kids or others to whom you give gifts.

o And don't forget Mother's Day, another day to treat your mom to a hygge experience!

Summer: The Outdoors is Ours

Since every time of year is a time for hygge and since summer is the time for vacation, relaxation, and outdoor activities, you might say that this is the most hyggelige time of the year - outside of winter. Most people take some time off in the summer, and it is certainly the time of year for lots of friendly outside gatherings with fun and sun. It may not be cozy socks and blankets, but that doesn't mean that you can't hygge up your outdoor spaces and your indoor activities.

o Lighten up your linens so you feel free to luxuriate in bed all morning long. In fact, why not treat yourself - or a loved one - to breakfast in bed? Make your bedroom a bright and welcoming space for exactly the kind of re-charging relaxation we could all use at any time of the year.

o Use your sunroom - or make one, as best you can. Create a hyggekrog that gets the best sunlight and set up a comfy couch or lazy lounge chair in there with plenty of throw pillows, cushions, and natural lighting. This is the place to catch up on summer reading.

o Speaking of summer reading, this is the time of year to indulge yourself in light, breezy reading, whatever that means to you: romantic comedies, mysteries, memoirs. Leave the studying to another time of year.

o Experience backyard living as much as you can: make a space in your backyard where everyone feels comfortable gravitating toward. Make sure there are cozy seats, enough for everyone, and natural décor for all to enjoy.

o Dine outside, of course, in your cozy backyard space, weather and bugs permitting. Put out some citronella to help with bugs to make it a safe space for everyone.

o Put up a hammock and set out some deck chairs, because this is the time of year to lounge - preferably with a nice cup of tea or glass of wine. Part of the hygge spirit is to slow down and enjoy every day; this is the perfect environment in which to do just that.

o Go camping and toast hot dogs and marshmallows around the campfire with your friends and family. If you're lucky, you'll have a beach nearby where you can enjoy a sunny day of fun and play followed by a warm night of good conversation and glorious summertime food.

o Pick up shells along the beach and make a garland or a necklace or a centerpiece for your dining table back at home.

o If you can, take a vacation. Better yet – and even more hyggelige – take a staycation, turning your home into a weekend or week-long getaway.

o Finally, remember a key component of the hygge philosophy: it's not about the financial investment; it's about the experience itself.

Festival of Days, from Memorial to Labor

Summertime is also rife with potential celebratory holidays, most of them secular holidays enjoyed by most Americans. Memorial Day, at the end of May, semi-officially kicks off the summer season, followed by Father's Day in June and Independence Day in July. The summer season semi-officially ends with the Labor Day holiday at the beginning of September. Obviously, these celebrations are American-centric; however, any excuse to host a celebration or to practice hygge with family and friends is nearly always a good one. Consider some of the following ideas on how to hygge-fy your summer holidays:

o Memorial Day is primarily a day of remembrance for fallen soldiers and veterans who have sacrificed much for our country; it is in the spirit of gratitude that we should approach the day. It is also the perfect time of year, weather-wise, to commune with family and friends at an outdoor gathering, usually a backyard barbecue. Spend the day putting flags and flowers at gravesites, attend a service for veterans, and/or visit your own family and friends who are veterans - this spirit of gratitude is very hygge. Then, spend the evening bonding with family and friends at a big backyard party, utilizing some of the tips mentioned above.

o Father's Day is also a day to express gratitude toward fathers who raised and mentored you. Remember that we may all have more than our biological fathers to honor on a day like this; perhaps a cherish grandfather or uncle, an adoptive father or stepfather, or an important mentor. Make a homemade card or gift to send your father figure(s) and be sure to let them know how much they mean to you. This can often take the form of another backyard barbecue or other kind of family gathering where the food is simple, and the company is grand.

o Independence Day is a celebration of America's history and independence, and another chance to express gratitude. It is also a chance to spend some time with family and friends and good food. Fireworks are perhaps a bit flashy for the normally subdued spirit of hygge, but in this case, the exuberance is well-placed. To make the fourth more hyggelige, give yourself a day at the beach, some time to reflect, and gather together with others in celebration. Also, grill some hygge food, like burgers and ribs!

o Labor Day honors the hard work that we all put in throughout the year. You could easily argue that, if hygge were a more ingrained part of American culture, we wouldn't need a Labor Day holiday at all - every day would be a way to enjoy work-life balance. In any case, note that Labor Day is the end of one season and the beginning of another, usually busier, time of year. Honor this by reminding yourself that hygge practice can be followed throughout the year, even with school starting back up and the lazy days of summer over. The Labor Day holiday is the perfect time to commit yourself to the practice of hygge through the fall and into the glorious winter. It's also another wonderful excuse to drag out the grill for one last outdoor shebang.

Fall: Cozy Up

While fall can seem to some like the end of the extended vacation that is summer, for others - and that means us, with our hyggelige vision - it can represent the long, slow slide into the coziest of seasons. Fall weather is crisp, and we start to bring out our oversize sweaters and cozy socks. Fall colors are naturally beautiful, so we incorporate those into our home décor. Fall evenings are muted and calm, perfect for postprandial strolls. Fall is the season when shops begin to close up earlier, bringing us back into the safe havens of our homes. It's one of the loveliest times of the year. Some uniquely fall activities and ideas to bring more hygge into your season are listed below.

o Do some fall planting: there are many crops and plants that like to spend the winter cozying up underground, so here is your last opportunity of the year to get your hands dirty in the yard and garden! Tulips are one such flower that likes to overwinter and are a beautiful symbol of spring. If you like vegetable gardens, then planting tubers and other root vegetables is the thing to do. Overwintering garlic is one of the most enjoyable - and simplest - kind of planting to do!

o Think of the symbol of the cornucopia: fall is the time to show gratitude for abundance, the prolific harvest. Do some canning and preserving - don't waste the end-of-season abundance that you have all around you. Share your bounty with family, friends, and neighbors.

o Go apple picking; get the family outdoors to enjoy the perfect time of year for this most symbolic of fruits. Have an apple bobbing contest later that evening, make some caramel apples for a divine fall treat - or both.

o Take a road trip to enjoy the changing of the seasons and the outburst of fall colors. Be sure to pack a picnic or two for along the way and sit under a tree while you watch the leaves gently drift to the ground.

o Welcome the pumpkin: one of the enduring symbols of fall, pumpkin and various other squash really come into their own this time of year. Aside from the whole jack-o-lantern business, you can also make pumpkin bread, pie, soup, and a whole host of other hyggelige recipes designed to make the best out of this hallowed vegetable.

o Start your knitting or learn how: this is the time of year to start on your projects for winter and gift-giving season. More on this in Chapter 10.

o Fall is also a wonderful time of year to take some photographs out in nature; the light is just right on most days, and the beautiful colors create gorgeous photos.

o Host a scavenger hunt! Cleverer and more adult than Halloween, a scavenger hunt is the perfect fall activity for a group of game friends. Get outside, have some fun, then be sure to offer some big bowls of soup and hunks of crusty bread to enjoy - along with good conversation - at the end of the evening.

Thanksgiving Is Not Just for Americans

The fall season isn't as rife with holidays, secular or otherwise, as the other seasons. For Americans, Thanksgiving holds great importance: it is both a nationally celebrated holiday that crosses all religious and cultural lines, as well as official start to the grand holiday season that is winter. Even if you aren't American - or if you find the myth of Thanksgiving a little too whitewashed for your taste - you can still appreciate the underlying message of giving thanks for all that we have enjoyed throughout the year. For most Americans, Thanksgiving means certain foods and family gatherings, and that is certainly in the spirit of hygge, as well: tradition and gratitude are key components of living the hygge lifestyle. So, roast your turkey and stuffing, if you like, or simply have friends and family over for a potluck dinner. Either way, you are practicing the greatest simple joys of hygge.

Chapter 8: Practical Hygge: Hygge Parenting, Relationships, and Togetherness

One of the most crucial components in practicing hygge is to encourage and facilitate positive relationships, fostering togetherness. Practicing hygge can have a profound impact on all your relationships, from parenting with empathy to nurturing a spousal bond to becoming a better friend. The hyggelige traditions of communing in cafes and eating family dinners around a set table together create bonds of affection that are lifelong. Hygge activities also emphasize the importance of spending time with our loved ones with joy and attentiveness. Embracing the simplicity and pleasure of every day is profoundly comforting to all of us - especially children - and recognizing that our highest forms of happiness come from our relationships with others remains at the core of the hygge way of life.

Parents: Parenting Peacefully

The impact that we have as parents cannot be overstated, of course, and the way that we decide to parent not only affects the physical and psychological health of our children but it also serves as a model for how our children behave and interact with others out in the world. Eventually, in most cases, this transfers to how your children parent their own kids. The hygge way of parenting emphasizes togetherness, authenticity, and empathy. It may seem, at first glance, that the hygge lifestyle is for the carefree and childless: afternoons spent lounging in cafes or in front of a fire or reading binges in a cozy and quiet corner. Yet, the underlying values inherent to the concept of hygge can be applied quite appropriately to parenting styles. Who among us wouldn't embrace the idea of "peaceful parenting?" It may sound easier said than done, but with a few thoughtful tips and techniques, you can incorporate the best of hygge into your parenting style.

o One of the most important parenting techniques you can employ is that of being present with your children. Tune in to their needs and wants, rather than trying to project onto them what you think they might need or want. Get down on their level - literally - and see the world through their eyes

o Be sincere and authentic when responding to their interests. Any child of reasonable acuity knows when an adult condescends to them, so respond with genuine questions and support.

o Empathy is also a central tenant in hygge-style parenting (and living, in general); fostering an empathy of others by demonstrating this to your own children creates a bond like no other.

o Encourage creative activity: get involved in art projects with your children or play dress-up or make-believe. Nurture their imagination and create a safe space for them to express themselves. Believe it or not, you will gain as much from this interaction as they do.

o Encourage play that is stimulating to the senses. While technological devices and computers have a place in our lives, to be sure, there is something to be said for more traditional kinds of tactile play. Consider investing in a sandbox, make models, or play with dough.

o Music is also an excellent way to get kids - and yourself - up and moving, while stimulating our bodies and minds. Physical activity is as important to brain development and overall health as is intellectual pursuits.

o Always eat together and encourage your children to participate. This ritual cannot be stressed enough! This habit of spending time preparing food, giving thanks, and eating around a table together is a habit for life. Study after study shows the amazing benefits that this one simple ritual can have on children. It makes for more humane, empathetic, and grateful interactions for the rest of their lives.

o Playing games together is another key component in fostering a child into adulthood. Games often provide practice for real life - at least in traditional games. With this in mind, try weaning kids away from the phone and the computer, engaging them in other forms of play that help them to model relationships and activities that will assist them in adulthood.

o Don't forget to play outside, as well. Nurture a love of the outdoors and empathy for nature, in general. Remember the Danish saying: there is no bad weather, only bad clothing choices. Outdoor play is a year-round affair, and in any season, there is always the reward of returning to the safe haven of the home, either for a mug of cocoa and a bowl of soup or for some lemonade and a smørrebrød spread.

o Read together - another surefire way to create a lifelong, positive habit! Encourage children to spend quiet time reading along, as well. Allow children the space to figure out their own self-care.

o Spend some time with physical affection, too. Snuggling and comforting your children is one the most significant things you can do to make them feel safe and happy throughout their lives. When you give them your full attention and engagement, you give them peace and happiness.

o Finally, remember to believe in yourself: trusting your hygge instincts as a parent will give you the confidence, kindness, and patience to nurture your children with love and generosity.

Partners: Nurturing Relationships

We would also do well to consider the foundations of a hygge lifestyle when approaching our partners, whether they are spouses, significant others, or co-parents. We often forget that relationships take effort, just as raising children to do. Without the same kind of nurturing spirit with which we approach our children, relationships can stagnate or grow untenable. The concept of hygge is easily applicable to our romantic relationships, and many of the basic tenants of hygge in and of themselves will foster a healthy connection. For example, creating a comforting and cozy home is a first step toward coming home from work into a welcoming environment, the kind of place where a good mood is easy to come by. Other tips and techniques for maintaining happy love relationships are as follows.

o Create good energy throughout your house, especially the places in which you interact at an intimate level, such as the bedroom. The living area is for everyone who enters your house, but the bedroom should be a place that is hygge-fied just for the two of you.

o Fill your home with items that have meaning, rather than material objects that simply advertise wealth or success.

You can't buy hygge; instead, you build it via memory-making and attention to the mundane details of the everyday. Family photographs, mementos from vacations, natural found objects decorate your space in such a way that cements togetherness.

o But don't forget yourself. One of the foundational elements in creating a hygge relationship is to embody hygge ideals yourself. Self-care is necessary in order to care for anyone else. Also, think of this in terms of your house: it should remind you not only of your present togetherness, but also of your individual self. Losing yourself in a relationship is not a formula for happiness, but rather a recipe for long-term resentments.

o Communication, as we all well know, is key to any constructive relationship. Learn to communicate openly, honestly, authentically, and calmly for best results.

o Cooperation is also key to any successful relationship, especially if it involves multiple people and objectives: partners raising children together invariably must cooperate on many fronts, but you also must learn to cooperate within the confines of your one interpersonal relationship. This is reliant on open and honest communication and a desire to put togetherness ahead of other goals.

o Leave work at work. This is harder to do than it sounds for many, if not most of us. However, if you are to create a relationship with true togetherness that embodies the spirit of hygge, then you must pay attention to the ways in which your working life invades your home life. Try to achieve as much balance as you can, and if you simply must address work issues at the home, try to follow some simple rules. Do not interrupt family time around the dinner table with work. Designate a specific area of the house - *not* the bedroom - in which work might be briefly conducted. Finish any work at least an hour before you plan to get to sleep, so you won't sacrifice evening bonding.

o Speaking of dinner, that time is a sacred time, something to be protected and honored. Make it a habit to keep it sacred.

o Use music to set the mood: curate your own playlists for different occasions, different seasons to keep you in the spirit of relaxed happiness.

o Slowing down, in general, is the rule of thumb when practicing hygge. Make special time for your significant other daily, no matter how seemingly simple or limited this might be. Hold hands while watching a movie, take a walk after dinner, commit to an hour before bedtime alone without interruption.

o Minimize the excess stuff in your lives, whether it is material or emotional. The baggage of all kinds interferes with peace and happiness.

Friends: Establishing Bonds

Another crucial factor in practicing hygge is to form and maintain friendship bonds. Besides your family, friends are the most important connections you have in the world, and ideally, friends fulfill needs that family cannot. Talking to a friend about the stresses you have in raising children is quite different than having that same discussion with a co-parent. Having some time away from family is just as healthy and important as spending quality time with them. Friendships are our way of keeping a sense of our own self separate from the needs and desires of family members. And, just as with children and with intimate relationships, friendships must be nurtured and cultivated with warmth and attention to maintain. One of the most striking facts to emerge out of recent sociological research is that social connection is the best predictor of overall happiness. Thus, we need to establish and maintain the bonds we have with our strongest social connections via friendships and other extended relationships.

o Make time to spend with friends on a regular basis. It's wonderful if you can establish a standing date and time to meet with friends each week or create a ritual in which friendly interactions take place with spontaneity and ease. The café culture in Denmark creates a kind of built-in experience in which to foster friendships; if you don't have that kind of thing where you live, think of other places/ways in which friendly meetings can happen (a diner, a bookshop, a casual bar).

o Invest in friendships by welcoming them into your home: host a monthly Sunday brunch, or Saturday game night, or Friday night card game, or wine Wednesdays, or thirsty Thursdays - whatever works best for your crowd. The point is to make the event a recurring one rather than an occasional one; planning and fuss are kept to a minimum, and your house becomes the welcoming, comforting place to be.

o Encourage drop-ins. This is not a typically American attitude in our contemporary society, where we often don't even know our neighbors, but this is an ingrained part of Danish life. If your home is hygge-fied, then you may find that it happens anyway.

o Don't worry about throwing big, elaborate parties in order to bond with friends. Oftentimes, the most intimate bonding happens with just a handful of people, ideally being three to five. Also, this isn't the point of hyggelige togetherness anyway; the point is to be relaxed, a comfortable, and casual wherein great company can be readily enjoyed.

o But do always have good food and drinks on hand. This doesn't have to be fancy, to reiterate, but in the spirit of hospitality, honor your friends with generosity and kindness.

o Savor the moment: envision time with friends as you would time with family, a time to unplug from devices and to interact with conviviality and conversation.

o Remember that friendship is a choice, unlike family, and with those choices come a dedication to caring for others outside of your immediate family. This kind of thinking has a definite ripple effect, radiating out from family to friends to neighbors to strangers. Fostering mutual respect and empathetic connection among peoples is at the heart of practicing hygge.

Family: Intergenerational Togetherness

Everything that can be said above about friendship and most of what can be said about our family relationships also applies to extended family. One of the tragedies of modern American life is that we spend more time with technology than ever and less time with our extended families and elders. So much wisdom is to be gained from maintaining relationships and connection with our grandparents, aunts, uncles, mentors, and others. While this is certainly not relegated just to hygge practice, the relationships that we can foster with extended family members enrich, enlighten, and enliven our lives in innumerable ways.

A story that might illustrate this better than any is that of a young woman who was going off to college, only to find that her scholarships didn't quite cover the cost of living on campus. Her grandmother lived nearby, but the prospect of spending her undergraduate years in her grandmother's home was not the most appealing - this wasn't how she envisioned college, for sure! Having no alternative, though, she acquiesced and moved her stuff into the guest room in the back. It was difficult at first, for though she had always spent time with this grandmother growing up, she had never been particularly close to her. Unlike her other grandmother, who doted on her and did grandmotherly things like baking and crafts, this grandmother was more interested in friends, cards, and adult conversation.

Much to her surprise when, gradually over time, she began to understand where her grandmother had come from: a rural and very poor background during which her father died young, leaving her uneducated mother to raise five children on her own. She learned that her grandmother had to take work as a young woman, foregoing further education, to support herself, and fell in love with an older man - her grandfather - who had old-fashioned ideas about women working outside the house. Her grandmother, she came to discover, was a wicked smart and fun-loving person who had never been afforded the opportunities in life to develop all she could have been. Instead, she now spent her days tirelessly supporting her granddaughter's endeavors to achieve all that she had been denied.

It dawned on the granddaughter one day that her grandmother was no mere grandmother: she was a mentor, a protective mothering figure, and a best friend. That relationship impacted the way she would view relationships from there on, with empathy and joy in the discovery of connection where it didn't seem that one could exist. That was the hygge spirit of the grandmother: she took pleasure in the small things in life, cooked with gusto, welcomed with open arms, and fostered love and happiness in all those she cared for. It would do us all good to take some time to foster those kinds of connections with our elders, if for nothing else than to teach us how to embrace hygge practice in the face of anything the world throws at   us.

Chapter 9: Practical Hygge: Frugal Hygge

It has been stated repeatedly throughout this book that practicing hygge does not require lavish expenditures. It is not about money; it is about the experience. Indeed, one of the very tenants of hygge is to avoid waste and enjoy what exists within the realm of your daily life - simplicity, simplicity, simplicity! Beyond this, however, there are ways to think about hygge as the happiest kind of frugal life you can lead. Anyone can practice hygge, no matter what their income and certain activities that are inherently hygge are also inherently budget-friendly. Check out some money-saving tips for how to hygge well and within a budget.

The Checklist

✓ What about all those candles? First, don't spend a fortune on them, whatever you do! It's hard to practice hygge right without them, and you'll inevitably burn through many, especially in winter. Shop the discount section of department stores for good bargains or seek out places where you can buy in bulk. Oftentimes, tea light and votive candles are a mere few cents each. In addition, eating (or living) by candlelight will invariably save you money on your electric bill. Marshalls™ always has a nice selection of candles and other hyggelige items - blankets, throw pillows, and the like - for reasonable prices. Wayfair.com is an online source for buying candles in bulk for more than half off-retail prices.

✓ What is one of the most hyggelige activities you can do? *Stay at home.* You don't need to seek out entertainment and transportation. Invite friends over for drinks and a movie, no expensive cocktails or Uber required unless those friends are having more than one or two drinks and intend to drive home. One of the core concepts of hygge is to be cozy, comfortable, and happy inside your own home.

✓ While you're at home, light up the fireplace or fire pit: this is an excellent way to stay warm and cozy for not a lot of money. Again, you are saving on gas or electricity while creating a cozy atmosphere for everyone to enjoy.

✓ Invest in just a few good, sturdy mugs for drinks at home with friends - coffee, cocoa, glogg, mulled wine, cider, and so on are all lovely in a plain old mug. Again, buy in bulk (inevitably, one or two will get broken), and don't worry about fancy labels or delicate china. Something that will easily go into the dishwasher and feel warm and solid in your hands suits the bill perfectly. This is a good way to get started with creating a hygge feeling on a limited budget. Worry about the other pieces as you are able.

✓ Decorate with natural and/or "found" objects. There is no need to spend a lot of money - or any, really - to create a hygge aesthetic in your home. Branches, pebbles, dried flowers and leaves arranged and displayed nicely are all you need to bring a little hygge home. All the better if you "craft" them up a bit. See the next chapter for some more ideas on crafting.

✓ Homemade is very definitely hygge, from food to décor to gifts to socks and scarves. Yes, it takes money to garner the supplies, but it is far less expensive to cook a homemade meal for four than it is to buy it! The same is true for decorative items and well-crafted gifts. Besides, a beautiful hand-drawn card is a keepsake, not just another throwaway for the landfill. You can also customize cheaper store-bought items for a personal touch either for your home or as a gift: throw pillows, cushions, blankets can all easily be gussied up with your own personal style. Learn to knit (or invest in a cheater kit), as yarn and knitting needles are far less expensive than buying scarves and hats and so on.

✓ Even if you aren't a very crafty person, you can still write a letter or send a thank you note. Gratitude is at the core of the hygge way of life, as well, and taking time out of your day for thanks is a frugal way to add some goodness to the world.

✓ Remember reading: talk about a frugal hygge thrill. Check out books from the library or scour used bookshops to buy plenty of fun and interesting reads. Encourage your friends to borrow and exchange books to widen your repertoire, as well. Start a book club and invite members to your warm and cozy house to talk books and sip mulled wine in front of the hearth.

✓ Take stock of what you need rather than what you desire. Hygge is about returning to simple values and simple pleasures, and we all get caught up in the constant striving of consumer culture at times. One of the most frugal activities you can do is to take inventory of what you have and how much of it you use. It won't take long for you to begin to clearly decide what is necessary and what is clutter. In addition, this gives you the opportunity to re-purpose certain items that you have. As the cliché goes: "One man's trash is another man's treasure." You might find hidden treasures stuffed in the back of your closet. With a little housecleaning effort, you may be able to hygge up your house with virtually no additional expenditure.

✓ Short of that, seek out used items for your hygge needs. Thrift stores and online warehouses offer lots of very affordable items, from comfy sweaters to great reads to household goods. For larger items, such as sofas or other furniture, Craigslist is always a solid option. In fact, the idea of recycling, of avoiding waste is central to the hygge philosophy and Scandinavian society in general.

✓ Start a savings account: if you discover that you lack several things that you'd like to have to refine your hygge lifestyle, or if you're just starting out, then start a hygge account for those things. Putting aside a bit from each paycheck will allow you to afford pieces little by little. Having a savings account is a pretty good idea, anyway.

✓ Also, remember that you don't have to do everything all at once. Start with one area of your life or home to begin practicing hygge. If you have a bike, then bike to the park - that's a start. If you want to start having friends over for game nights, then hygge up your living room - bedrooms and baths and wardrobe can wait. Take it one piece at a time, and remind yourself that hygge is a mindset, really, not a bunch of material things.

✓ The simple things are often the best things in life, as well. It doesn't cost anything to spend some time snuggling with a loved one or looking through old pictures for a reminiscence costs absolutely nothing and means just about everything. Spending time with loved ones is infinitely better than spending money.

Chapter 10: Practical Hygge: Hygge Crafts

As has been mentioned frequently throughout the book, homemade and hand-crafted are most certainly at the heart of hygge practice. Not only does this encapsulate the spirit of the simple, slowed-down lifestyle, it also emphasizes both frugality and generosity. The frugality of crafting items from raw materials - always cheaper than buying mass-produced, factory-made goods - balanced with the expression of heartfelt generosity that is embodied in each handmade item you create is one of the deepest hallmarks of hygge practice. A handmade card with a thoughtful personal note is infinitely more hygge than a department store purchase; A lovely centerpiece made from found objects and natural materials is stunning in a way that a bought showpiece can never be. Wearing hats, scarves, and sweaters knitted by hand showcases the essence of hygge practice - cozy and caring, comfortable and generous. Happiness is but a quiet moment of thoughtful labor and an enduring satisfaction at creating joy for yourself and others with your own two hands.

Some general ideas of what kind of crafts are especially hygge follow, along with some specific suggestions for projects you could undertake in the Checklist section.

o Remember that one of the key components to crafting in a hyggelige way is to savor the process. Sit back in your hyggekrog and relax into the gentle labors of knitting a quilt or stitching a sweater - or any other of the craft ideas to follow. Take pleasure in the soothing process of slowing down and embracing a task that our busy world has nearly forgotten. The end results are nothing short of the physical embodiment of the cozy, happy spirit of hygge.

o When embarking on household projects - especially if you are new to the concept of crafting - think small and manageable. Instead of starting out knitting a sweater, think about adding some texture to a sweater or cardigan you already have. Adding texture to household items or wardrobe pieces is another hallmark of hygge. Learning to stitch a small but meaningful decoration on a beloved sweater is a way to accomplish both textural interest and the hyggelige joys of the homemade and personal.

o Don't get bogged down in the big things, especially when it comes to hygge-fying your household. It may feel overwhelming to add large pieces of furniture, create a fireplace and hearth where none existed before, or to repaint a room or replace carpet. Those are big - *and sometimes expensive* – undertakings! In hygge, it's the little things that matter, the small and simple things that add spark to your home. A hand-painted vase or paper-made baubles, a decorative wreath made of natural materials or a small sampler for a throw pillow: these are the things that make your home cozy, comfortable, and meaningful.

o Think of practicing crafting as expanding the hygge tenant of fostering relationships: handmade gifts are ever-so-thoughtful and warm the hearts of both the giver and the recipient. Even if you purchase a present for someone, you can personalize it with a handmade card or a cross-stitch tag. It is the little touches that can ultimately make the difference between a mediocre and memorable gift.

o While we don't always associate the art of cooking as a craft, it most certainly is! Even though a culinary gift may be ephemeral, it is truly from the heart. The breaking of bread together is one of the most ancient and revered of all social interactions, and feeding people is expressing love in the most intimate of ways. Baking bread for a neighbor or friend - providing a handwritten recipe card with it - is one of the most hygge crafts in which you can indulge. At the holidays, baking of all types is a lovely way to spend a cold winter morning, while having the added satisfaction of providing cheerful - and yummy - sustenance to family and friends. A festive bag of various holiday cookies is a present par excellence.

o Remember those candles? So important to hygge, candles and candlelight are at the very root of how to hygge in your home - and, *they can also be handmade.* For just a small initial investment in materials, you can customize candles - size, shape, scent - for yourself and your family and friends. It's also another element of the frugal nature of hygge, as homemade candles, in the long run, are less expensive than buying them, and recycling all the bits of wax left at the end of a candle's life leaves you with material to begin again!

o Another craft idea that has been mentioned throughout the book is using natural materials in your household décor. It can be as simple as layering items in a clear jar or vase or as complicated as creating a pattern out of dried flowers to decorate a gift box. You can also adorn your table with a centerpiece or your mantle with a garland of natural materials. Even high-end restaurants are getting in on this trend, festooning walls and arches with actual organic material. There are abundant ideas to be had all over the internet, as well as books specializing in crafting from nature.

o Certainly, as mentioned above, knitting is one of the central crafts to utilize the hygge spirit. It combines the use of soft, neutral materials with the ability to customize coziness via hats or scarves, sweaters, and afghans. While knitting is a skill that takes time to develop, there are some shortcut methods if you are a beginner. Weaving looms assist in doing the knitting for you. Consider embarking on smaller projects as you begin your hygge journey. While hygge may seem to call for the more traditional method, it certainly wouldn't forbid the beginner's learning curve. Even with the shortcut methods, there is the time spent in slowing down and creating with your hands.

o While many crafts are instinctual and improvisational, there are innumerable resources out there for you. Even the most experienced crafter can glean new ideas and hone old skills by picking up a well-respected book on crafting the hygge way.

The Checklist

Here are some specific ideas for actual crafting projects that you could undertake, from knitting, crocheting, and sewing to home décor and miscellaneous other ideas. These projects range from ideas for the advanced crafter to simple tasks for beginners. Read through the entire list for a variety of ideas. Don't hesitate! Get started on one of these immensely satisfying projects today.

✓ Pick out a knitting pattern for a hygge-style sweater. These patterns can be found in any local crafts store or in various places throughout the internet. Remember: a hand-knitted sweater isn't just a one-time gift, it's a precious keepsake to be passed down through the family.

✓ Looking for something simpler than a sweater? Pick out a knitting pattern for a plush hand-knit bag - perhaps the perfect place to keep your knitting materials all in one cozy place when you're done. This would also be a terrific gift for a knitting friend, or it could be a cute accessory for a crisp winter day.

✓ Or, you could tackle a quilting or blanket project. These patterns come available in the incredibly simple to incredibly complex: a cozy, chunky-knit afghan is possible to make in one mere day with some of these patterns. More complex items use a variety of materials, creating varying patterns and textures.

✓ Crocheting is another nearly lost art that creates the same cozy, comfy feel of knitting for a variety of projects. For example, crochet yourself (or a loved one) some warm slippers for wearing while reading a book by the fire.

✓ Or, you could crochet lovely cozies for your soup bowls or teapot or favorite mug. These custom-made cozies are guaranteed not only to keep your food and drink warm but also to make them aesthetically inviting. Practical and pretty, these are good project ideas for the beginning crochet aficionado.

✓ You can also use your crochet skills to make small handbags or clutches, creating tapestry-like patterns to make another practical and pretty item for your personal use.

✓ Pick out the very softest of yarns to crochet the ultimate scarf, the kind you'd like to nuzzle your face and hands into on the coldest of winter days. This is also a lovely gift idea for any friend or family member who enjoys the comforts of hygge.

✓ Since you're starting to get into the whole idea of crafting, why not crochet yourself a personalized pincushion to help with your pins and such while sewing? It's a small but meaningful project that will keep you coming back to your crafting for more, simply because it's an inviting symbol of accomplishment.

✓ There are also more complicated crocheting projects you can take on, such as crocheting an oversize poncho for use at the campfire, making it out of lighter material for the perfect accompaniment to an early spring picnic. Nice, chunky boot slippers are another way to hygge up your wardrobe via your own craftiness and don't forget the absolute usefulness of a lovely, handmade hat. Simple as they are, you can craft a hat for nearly every occasion.

✓ Don't forget about one of the other essential parts of your hygge wardrobe and sew yourself up a pair of comfy sweatpants. There are some relatively easy patterns out there for you to follow. Short of sewing a pair, embroider your own favorite pair with a lovely design or meaningful phrase.

✓ You could also apply sewing skills to other home items, such as pillowcases and decorative throws. Sewing a personal slipcover for a piece of furniture is also a nice project, as is creating personalized table linens, such as tablecloths, placemats, and napkins, either via adding decorative details or creating from scratch.

✓ Don't forget the quilting tradition: save bits of this and that, things that have personal meaning and importance, to create a keepsake for the ages. Involve your friends, too, for a very hyggelige quilting circle.

✓ There is also a northern tradition in the Scandinavian heart: these handmade hearts are made all over Scandinavia, sometimes a tradition attributed to the Danish author Hans Christian Andersen. These are particularly popular at Christmas. Often, they are very simple hearts made of paper, but the woven heart has a great following, as well. Making a few dozen of these to accompany packages at the holidays is a lovely way to start your own yearly tradition. Some specific ideas for home décor could include the following projects:

 o Use found pine cones to create a wreath. This could be crafted to hang on the wall or to serve as a centerpiece. With some consideration (i.e., avoid any fire danger), it could serve as a nest for a candle, as well.

o Make some candles, as mentioned above. Remember that you need barely invest anything in materials: save up bits of wax from various spent candles and repurpose them in a teacup for a whole new look.

o Make candle holders out of recycled and/or rustic materials. Burlap is an excellent material for this, for one example. Candle cozies have the additional benefit of muting the candle's glow for an even more hyggelige atmosphere, as well as adding a personal touch to your household décor.

o How do you store all those mugs you've collected for coffee, cocoa, and tea? You make a stand or a wall hook out of wood. Hang your mugs from a hand-crafted, wooden project for both practical purposes - they're all right there at your fingertips - and artful display.

o Speaking of displays, if you have the woodworking skills to craft these small projects, think of other places where you can put your crafting to both practical and pretty use. Consider crafting a mounted set of wall hooks for visitors to hang their coats and sweaters on, or a wooden tree or mount upon which to hang your jewelry in your bedroom. How about a simple box in which to store utensils or crafting materials? Just because something is practical doesn't suggest it shouldn't be meaningful.

o Make wall hangings out of natural materials. Your sewing, knitting, or crocheting skills could come in handy here, or you could seek out various pieces in the remainder bin at your local craft store, pulling together something unique and personal. Bits of fur, swatches of various materials, even repurposed clothing can be stitched together to bring a bit of hygge style to your home. Be sure to focus on neutral, calming colors for the more hyggelige look, rather than a riot of a mismatch.

o Make or customize your own photo frames. Using natural materials, you can craft your own frames for display throughout your house. This also makes for a wonderful gift. You could also customize frames by adding a bit of found natural material here and there - pick up and polish some sticks or stones in your own back yard - for something lovely and worthy of displaying your legacy.

o Don't forget about the seasons! Homemade Christmas ornaments are a wonderful addition to any tree, from small stained-glass projects to painted baubles to crocheted garland. All these things create a very hygge holiday. Make a winter village to display throughout the season, from clay and paint. Attend a pottery workshop to craft some holiday candle holders or vases, and so on. Craft a handmade advent calendar to count down the days until Christmas. Write your best holiday recipes on lovely notecards to give to friends and family. Knit or crochet stockings for the family or embroider stockings you already have with names or sayings of holiday cheer. Truly, the ideas are infinite, and there are innumerable books and guides available for you to find the perfect craft to round out your hygge holiday experience.

✓ Making a personalized scrapbook became a booming business about twenty years ago, and it remains a wonderful way for the beginning crafter to express love and gratitude toward family and friends. A fun way to think about scrapbooking is to tell a story using words, pictures, and decorative additions. Give your best friend a scrapbook for her 40th birthday or make a scrapbook to be completed for a mother-to-be or put together a scrapbook of inspirational sayings and images for an anniversary present or a college graduation gift. The possibilities are numerous and require minimal skill, just thoughtfulness and time.

✓ Essential oils are another hyggelige way that you can personalize your home. Another "craft" that takes minimal skill and only a few materials, you can create your own scents and diffusers to place strategically throughout the house.

✓ Speaking of scents, there are numerous crafty ideas to both decorate and aromatize your homes, such as drying herbs and/or flowers to be used in sachets for closets or drawers.

✓ Remember: mugs, tableware, and other household items can be homemade or customized, as well. There are classes available in many places that offer instruction on pottery and amateur glassmaking, as well as woodworking and metalworking. Some of these are quite advanced, but there is also any number of beginner's projects to tackle at first.

✓ Kitchen projects are another type of hygge crafting. Those going beyond the daily task of family meal making are especially in tune with the notion that homemade is better, engendering a greater spirit of generosity and a warm feeling of happiness. This feeling is for us, as givers, as much as for the recipients. Some potential projects and specific ideas to consider are as follows.

    o Canning: This is an ideal hyggelige craft if you have an abundant garden. This is not only a way to preserve your harvest, minimizing waste and maximizing frugality, but also a way to turn a glut of produce into a wonderful holiday gift. Think preserves and jams, pickles and sauces. A nearly foolproof way to preserve your harvest for months - even years - to come, canning is a lost art among most home cooks. Supermarkets have made it far too easy to obtain whatever produce you want at whatever time of year you desire it. While there is nothing inherently wrong with this, it's certainly economically and environmentally sound to grow your own food and to preserve it. Canning is a time-honored way to do just that.

o Freezing: if you don't have the time or space for the equipment required in canning, you can put your freezer to good use. While this may not be the ideal way to plan on future gift-giving, it is undoubtedly a lovely gift to give yourself and your family: thawing a bag of homemade tomato sauce in the depths of February is like unleashing a ray of sunshine. If you want to make it even simpler than sauce, simply roast some of your abundant tomatoes for a few minutes in a hot oven, then slip off the peels and toss them into a - carefully labeled - freezer bag. Then, throughout the non-growing season, you can pull these out and use them however you wish. Other good candidates for freezing are any abundant vegetables from your garden or local farmer's market that can be blanched quickly, laid out on cookie sheets to freeze individually, then stored in freezer bags for the winter: think green beans, sugar snap peas, asparagus, broccoli, and cauliflower. Again, this is a way to treat yourself to some lovely and healthy self-care during the non-growing season.

o Dehydrating is another way to preserve the produce of spring and summer, as well as having the side benefit of creating crafty ways to either scent or decorate your home. For example, if you end up with a glut of herbs, dehydrating these for future use is one of the best ways to use them up - and they smell lovely, as well, to add to a sachet or aromatic diffuser. For another example, if you have a glut of peppers, you can string these up on a *ristra* (or wreath) to dry. Not only can you use them in stews, soups, or sauces (or grind them for seasoning), but they also look beautiful in the kitchen.

o Pickling: a time-honored tradition of home cooks everywhere, homemade pickles make lovely gifts and thrifty projects. Fermented foods have made a comeback in recent years as the growing consensus suggests that the active cultures (or probiotics) in naturally fermented foods are remarkably good for our overall health, especially in maintaining a healthy digestive system. Pickles that you buy in the supermarket are typically heat-treated in some way or pickled using vinegar and not fermentation; both methods effectively kill any active microorganisms. Naturally fermented or "pickled" vegetables made at home contain a host of good probiotics if monitored carefully and taste superior to mass-produced items.

o There are other ways of using the kitchen as a craft center: making scented oils or vinegar for your own use or for gifts is a lovely way to customize a neutral oil. Use citrus peel and herbs, or garlic and spices for inspiration. Vinegar is especially good vehicles for infusing herbal essences, tarragon vinegar being a traditional condiment all over Europe. Don't forget the potent powers of alcohol, as well: distilling spirits at home isn't feasible, of course, but infusing neutral alcohol (usually vodka) with various flavors makes for a festive gift. Vanilla beans, citrus peels, peppercorns, and other aromatics make excellent candidates for a winter treat. You can also make your own liqueurs with various flavorings, some alcohol, and a bit of sugar. Homemade limoncello is easy, as is cinnamon or coffee liqueur. Make a big vat of mulled wine while you're at it, and seal into bottles with specialized labels to hand out to guests over the holidays. The kitchen is an ideal place to hone your hygge crafting abilities.

✓ Finally, it would do us good to remember that the spirit of hygge suggests that we take delight in every day, in the simple things, so that the very mundane tasks with which our lives are filled should give us cause for joy and a pause for gratitude. In that sense, cleaning and caring for loved ones, doing laundry or mowing the land, are crafts of daily love and comforting happiness.

Conclusion

The art of hygge is a simple one: immerse yourself in the warmth and comfort of your beautifully lit and naturally decorated house with good friends, hearty food, and some happy conversation. Ride your bike to the local café for some coffee and fika. Indulge in some serene self-care, curled up in your cozy nook with a good book and a warm drink. Hygge is about fostering a long-term sense of happiness and general well-being; material consumption and ambitious striving are ephemeral distractions that lead us not to happiness - but to hurriedness. Hygge gives us the opportunity to step back from our overly busy lives and instead, start to value the small, daily joys that we are surrounded by. It encourages us to be present in our own lives.

Philosophically speaking, hygge is about comfort and coziness, preferably in the spirit of fellowship and family. Practically speaking, hygge is about designing a lifestyle that is simple and serene, warm and happy.

With all the practical tips and ideas that you have discovered throughout this book, you should be able to devise a hygge lifestyle that both comforts you and keeps you happy. From the atmosphere within your home to the clothing you choose to wear, you can embrace all aspects of hygge. Strike up a fire, start up a slow-simmered stew, stir up a warm and soothing drink, and be sure to invite some friends! Hygge is more than a trend or a hard-to-pronounce word; it is an immensely satisfying way of life that has engendered the happiness of millions. Now you can count yourself one of them.

Part 2: Lagom

What You Need to Know About the Swedish Art of Living a Balanced Life

Introduction

The following chapters will discuss the Swedish secret to happy and fulfilling lives. It may go against a lot of what we value and are used to in our American culture, but with so many people searching for something more, something that will help to bring about more happiness, it could be just what you are looking for.

In this guidebook, we are going to spend some time looking at the Swedish lifestyle of lagom (pronounced "lah-gome"). This is a word that means "just enough". You do not want to have too much of something, but you do not want to go so much to the extreme that you will not be able to enjoy life either. With lagom, there are no extremes, we get just enough of everything that we want or need, and this leads to a happier and healthier life than ever before.

We are going to start out this guidebook by looking at what lagom is all about, and how it is meant to work. We will look at how you can add in "just enough" to your day and your life, and still gain so much more happiness than you would have ever imagined in the past. We will also spend some time looking at the benefits that come with lagom and why so many people are deciding to adopt the Swedish way of life into their own lives as well.

Once we have a better understanding of how lagom works and why it is so beneficial, it is time to dive further in and look at some of the different ways that you can add this into your own life. Lagom can be added into every part of your life, though this can seem a bit overwhelming to some people (just jumping right in), especially when they are used to the American consumerist lifestyle.

Therefore, it is perfectly fine to start out with lagom slowly. You can add it into one or two aspects of your life and notice a big improvement. When you are ready, and you see all the great benefits, you can easily add it into other aspects of your life, as you are ready. Along the way, this guidebook will provide you with the information that you need to really add Lagom to areas like your home, your work, your relationships, your food, your clothing, and even your style of parenting.

When you are ready to learn more about the Swedish philosophy of lagom, and you are ready to simplify your life to add in more happiness, make sure to continue reading this guidebook and learn more about how to get started.

Chapter 1: What is Lagom?

There are many different types of lifestyles that are encouraged throughout the world. And people, in different countries and with different backgrounds, may take life at a different pace than the rest of us. While Americans may seem to be moving faster and faster every day while feeling drained and like they have missed out on friendships and other things that are important, you will find that many countries, and even many people within this country, have decided to make a switch as well.

To start, we need to explore the ideas behind minimalism. Minimalism - which is basically the art of having less - is a big trend that has made its way into many different aspects of our lives including our home, our work, food, apparel, and so much more. We find that we may meal prep with fewer and more basic ingredients because it saves time and money. We learn how to cut down what is in our wardrobes to help make decisions easier and to reduce the footprint we are leaving on the planet. We stop buying as much stuff that we do not need so that our homes will not feel as cluttered in the long run.

While most of us understand what minimalism is all about and how it is meant to work. While consuming less is going to make us feel less debt to an item, we also need to explore more about this topic.

Especially, we need to look at what minimalism means to other people, or what lagom means to other countries.

This brings us to our discussion of lagom. Lagom is going to be the Swedish art of balanced living. We can translate this word to being "not too little, not too much, just right." This may sound confusing, but it is a good way to help us stay busy and not become lazy, without having to take on too much in our work life, our home lives, and in all of the other aspects that seem to surround us on a daily basis.

As someone who is already a minimalist (or is at least thinking about becoming a minimalist), it is important to always do an evaluation of what is around you to see how much you can live without and still be comfortable, and even see what you are able to live without or how to live with less. The question here is: what if the issue we are facing is not continuing to eliminate or hoard? What it is more about finding the equilibrium that is perfect for our lifestyles without having to cause a lack or an excess in the process?

The idea behind lagom is not that you want to try to reach perfection. Instead, it is all about finding a simple and attainable kind of solution to the daily worries that you go through. This could include things like making sure you have enough downtime, eating better, reducing the amount of stress that you have, and even achieving more happiness. It is going to help us to learn how to balance work and life so that we can sustain it all and have them all exist harmoniously with one another.

This seems like a pretty practical and worthwhile kind of solution to our busy world, right? There are a lot of different things that you are able to do with this lifestyle choice, and we are going to explore a few of them throughout this guidebook. You will be learning more about what lagom is all about and why it is such a good option. The suggestions made in this book change be adapted in various manners to ensure that it works for your own lifestyle.

According to Linnea Dunne, the author of *Lagom: The Swedish Art of Balanced Living,* some of the different things that you can do in order to make sure that you are living this kind of lifestyle include working with ethical clothing, eating locally, trying to grow some of your own food, taking more breaks through the day to feel rested, and so on.

The thing to remember when you are working with lagom is that there are going to shift in our days and sometimes, no matter how hard we try, we are not going to be able to fit it in everywhere. This is part of the beauty of living lagom: if you cannot check everything off the list each day, that is not a big deal. Just keep the fuss out of the whole situation and make your day as fulfilling and relaxing as you can.

With lagom, you need to make sure that your aim is to have a fuss-free lifestyle. This means that we need to learn how to find contentment and pleasure in the things that we already have, even if what we have is not picture-perfect. Also, make your goal to understand how all the things that we do play an important part in how we are going to live a life that is less destructive, and more sustainable, on this earth.

Not everyone who decides to embrace the idea of lagom wants to be able to adopt it on a daily basis, doing it all of the time. It is easy to admit that going with a lifestyle that is free of all the stress and fuss probably sounds pretty ideal. In a culture where over-indulgence is going to be the norm and you are looked down on if you are not able to keep up with what the neighbors have, it is nice to think that there are many other methods that you can rely on. Lagom shows you how to sit back and relax, live with less stuff, and actually enjoy the life that you are living now.

When you first hear about this term, you may assume that it is the same as the popular "hygge" that was available a few years ago. It was almost impossible to head out anywhere or even enter a bookstore without seeing a lot of information on the Norwegian and

Danish word that meant coziness. There will be some similarities occurring between two ideas; hopefully you will be able to see through this guidebook that the lagom ideology is going to be a bit different.

While this term is going to seem similar, there are going to be some key differences. First off, hygge is going to be about coziness and being comfortable, and lagom is more about "just the right amount." The basic idea that comes with this lifestyle philosophy is that we need to find a good harmonious balance and the right amount of happiness. The goal is not having too much, but also not having too little in your life.

On its surface, hygge is more about taking time out and making sure that you always feel safe and cozy. Of course, while these two ideas are going to be a bit different, we can see how both of them are going to be able to complement each other nicely, and if you have already implemented the ideas of hygge into your life, or you are looking to get happiness, comfort, and less stress in all aspects of your life, then combining the two together can be the right answer for you.

We will also spend some time looking at the history that comes with lagom. The Swedes believe that the best way for anyone to live a happy life, they must follow the precepts of lagom. You deprive yourself of nothing, but you also make sure that you are not overdoing things. Moderation is the key here, and it is the best way for you to create a life that is balanced and fulfilling.

In fact, this idea is so indoctrinated into the culture of Sweden that it is visible in all of the different aspects of their life, from their work-life to their homes, and you can even find this idea in their political system. Everyone in this culture should have enough, but not too much – that is the essential principle that the people of Sweden stick with, and it ends up working great for them and their happiness levels.

Lagom is unique in that it strikes a nice balance between hygge and minimalism. You do not need to be heated up by piles of cozy blankets or burn the house down with all your scented candles! Likewise, you do not need to feel like you can only own one spoon, throwing out all the other things that you own. This is where lagom is going to be the best option because it allows you to meet in the middle between these two lifestyle ideas.

This is a kind of lifestyle that works so well because it is going to help leak over into all of the areas of your life, and not just one or two. Having a good work and life balance, having just the right number of possessions, being able to reduce the amount of stress that you have, and keeping a healthy amount of frugality are all essential. It can even go all the way down to eating the right amount of food at mealtimes and choosing the right clothes.

With some of these ideas in mind, it is now time for us to learn a few of the simple methods that you are able to use in order to help improve your life and ensure that you are going to use the ideas of lagom a bit better. Some of the ways that you can work on adding some more lagom in your life will include the following:

Adopt What is Known as "Morgondopp"

The first thing that we need to explore doing when you would like to add more of lagom into your lifestyle is to adopt the "morgondopp". Think about the landscape that comes with Sweden. It has been blessed with more than 7000 miles of coastline and at least 100,000 lakes. Because of all this water and the coastline that is near it, it is no wonder that the Swedes love to bathe! One of these bathing types is going to stand out from the rest, and that is the morgondopp, or the morning dip.

This process is something that the Swedes are often going to enjoy this between May and September when it is warmer, but there are some who are going to do this all throughout the year. This kind of bath is enjoyed first thing in the morning before they even have their first cup of coffee. The bather dons a dressing gown, then wanders down to the local bathing deck.

The length of time that you decide to stay in the water is going to depend on the temperature. Many people will start when the water reaches 50 degrees. Then they will jump right in and let the water wake them up and make them more ready for the day. It can be a humbling experience, and it is going to be relaxing to feel the cool breeze and the warm sun on your body when you are all done with that morning bath!

So, what are you supposed to do if you do not live anywhere near a lake, stream, river, or sea? A good place to start here is to end the daily shower that you take with a cold-water blast. It may not give you quite the same feeling as a saltwater swim, but you will still get many of the physiological benefits as well. If nothing else, it is going to help wake you up with a nice jolt!

Dare to Go Alone

Sometimes when you are practicing lagom, it is fine to do some things on your own. This sounds strange to many cultures that are outside of Sweden. We feel like we always need to be surrounded by other people and that if we are doing something alone, then no one likes us, or perhaps there is something else wrong. With lagom, sometimes it is just fine to go out and explore the world and do things on your own, without having a ton of other people around.

Consider trying something small to help you get started. You do not have to go crazy here and assume that the only way you can succeed here is to go out for weeks on end camping and exploring the wilderness. If this is something that is appealing to you, go ahead and do it. But for the most part, you do not have to take things to this kind of extreme. For those used to being around others all the time, maybe going out on a short walk in nature by your home - on your own - can be a good place to start.

Work on Your own Capsule Wardrobe

Another idea that we are going to talk about in a little more detail as this guidebook goes on - and in another chapter - is the idea of the capsule wardrobe. Loosely speaking, the wardrobe that you will find of the average Swedish person is going to be likened to what would be a capsule wardrobe. This is going to be a minimalist, highly practical closet that was created by clearing out any of the unused and unwanted clothes and replacing them with a limited number of loved and highly versatile garments that you could mix, match, and wear together if you like.

There are several benefits to this. It saves money on buying clothes all the time. Moreover, it makes it easier to pick out an outfit in the morning, or any other time, taking some of the stress out of your morning. In addition, it helps you to spend less time and energy on things like shopping and laundry. It is more economical, and those who decide to go with it are often going to feel so much happier in the long run.

Take Enough Breaks in Your Day

The Swedish time of fika-paus is a break with some coffee and sometimes a little treat. It could be an informal kind of catch-up with a colleague that was prompted by something like "Shall we meet up at 10 a.m. and have coffee?" Alternatively, it could be something that is a bit more formal, an event that you scheduled out on the calendar a long time in advance for everyone to get together. Whether it is more of a formal or an informal thing, it is going to include taking some time to "turn off" and have a breather, even if it is just for a few minutes.

In our modern culture, it is easy to feel guilty when we are going to take a break, and when we try to relax from all of the hard work that we do. But it is actually something that is good for you and can make you more productive. A study that was done at Baylor University's Hankamer School of Business found that those who took more breaks when they were at work reported that they had more energy, that they were able to concentrate more, have more motivation, and they were less likely to report some of the negative side- effects such as lower back pain and headaches.

What is interesting here is that the positive effects that come with these breaks are going to decrease the more time that you work between the breaks. This is why taking some short and regular breaks is the key to seeing success. In fact, if you want to practice some lagom, you should follow something like the 52 – 17-minute rule.

A recent study supported this idea, finding that those who were the most productive would work for 52 minutes, and then they would get a 17-minute break. While this is not something that many jobs are going to allow, it is still worth it for us to think about the frequency of our breaks and try to take some as often as we can in between our work.

This does not mean that you must go and talk to someone each time and have a long conversation. If you are more introverted and the idea of going out to find someone to talk to ten times a day seems daunting, then do not fret. Even having some time alone and indulging in a break on your own, can work just as well and will provide you with the same kinds of benefits.

Learn How to Listen More

If you ever converse with someone from Sweden, and you will notice that they are not going to waste any time interrupting or talking over another person. They keep their voices at an even tone, and it is acceptable to have some pauses in the conversation if needed. To those in American and other cultures, this can seem awkward. Culturally, we are so concerned about a gap in the conversation that we are going to jump in too soon, often trying to speak talk before the other person complete their sentence.

But in lagom, the idea is to stop and actually listen to another person. This helps to slow down the discourse and allows both parties to really feel like they are being listened to. It is hard to follow through will allowing the conversation with pauses; it can make us feel uncomfortable, and sometimes makes the conversation seem unnatural. We have been told that this is the way that we are supposed to behave and that the conversation has to keep going.

It is acceptable if the conversation flows back and forth with no stopping; trying to force this without really listening to what your other person is saying can be so bad for the encounter! Allowing for some pauses, enabling both parties to hear and process what the other one is saying, is so important. After all, the point is for both parties to actually understand what the conversation is about.

Perform Acts of Kindness

As with all the other topics that we have discussed with lagom, spreading happiness is something that you can easily do, without having to involve a ton of grand gesture. Sometimes a small and ordinary act will be enough and will mean the most when it inspires someone to smile in their day.

Even though you may think that you are a very caring person already, sometimes a gentle reminder to think of others and to remember to do something kind for them can go a long way. In addition, catching another person off guard with a bit of kindness that they were not expecting can be one of the most touching gestures of all. Some of the different ideas that you might think about using in order to get the most out of these random acts of kindness can include:

1. Leave a small note in one of the books that you are reading at the library to brighten someone's day.
2. Decide to give out ten compliments to various people throughout the day, ones that are heartfelt and genuine.
3. Write a thank-you note to the public service industry, such as a nurse, firemen, or the police.

4. Write a letter to a relative or a friend you have not been in touch with for a long time.

5. Carry around an extra umbrella or something similar, providing it to a friend in when they need it.

Living a life that is full of lagom is going to help you to improve your daily existence and your happiness. As you can see in this guidebook, it is a lot easier to accomplish than you may have originally thought. Taking breaks, thinking about others, stopping to listen rather than just react, and enjoying life rather than buying things and having to work to pay them off, can be so freeing to your overall life.

Chapter 2: The Benefits of lagom and Why You Should Pursue It NOW!

There are going to be many great benefits that you can receive when you decide to implement some of the ideas of the lagom system into your own life. This is why so many people have chosen to add in this kind of ideology to their own lives, ensuring that they reach happiness and then continue having a good life. It is in stark contrast to what we usually see when we look at our modern world, where we are encouraged to run around at a breakneck speed and just keep purchasing things left and right. With lagom, we learn what is just enough, but not too much, and it can lead to so much more happiness than ever before. With this in mind, let's look at some of the benefits that you'll reap when you decide to implement some lagom - even if it is not full time - into your life:

You Can Take Yourself Away from the Extremes

In our modern culture, we seem to go back and forth between the extremes. We go with either diet or bingeing. We spend time doing daily hard workouts or watching marathons on Netflix. These extremes are going to make us feel really unhappy and exhausted, and it is hard to know which way to turn. But the goal with lagom is to find a good medium, the medium of *just enough*. Just enough for play and work. A healthy diet with a nice dessert to enjoy when supper is done. Watching a bit of TV and then a good exercise during the day.

The balance, rather than taking it all away and depriving ourselves, is the essential ingredient that we should strive to remember daily with lagom. If we spend our whole lives trying to deprive ourselves of the things we should and need to do, or the things that we enjoy, we are going to end up on burn-out. After burn-out, it's easy to head the other direction, swinging to the other side of the pendulum; this is not good for us either.

The best way for us to really describe what lagom is all about, in just a few words, is it is the happiest grey area ever! This is a nice grey area where you are going to feel fulfilled by working out just enough, eating just enough, sleeping enough, and getting out there and adventuring enough. Gluttony is not the best for us at all, but this does not mean that we need to starve ourselves either. Working out all of the time is hard on the mind and the body but sitting around and never moving at all is not good for our bodies either. The grey area allows us to have just enough of both to be happy.

You Are Going to be Happier

Happiness can only begin when you have had a chance to get those basic needs taken care of, and it is going to end with the love and the gratitude of what your life is and is becoming. When you begin adding some of the principles of lagom into your life, you will see the importance of making sure that the excess is gone, leaving room for more of the things that are wanted and needed. When things are just right, which is encouraged with the fundamentals and process of lagom, you are going to feel good.

Our goal here is to not aim for giddy or over-the-top joy that starts by burning bright and then ends up fizzling out quickly like a fire that is started by gasoline with nothing to sustain it. We are, instead, shooting to reach a deep amount of contentedness and the joy that can last your whole life. Lagom is going to help you to reach this long-lasting happiness, rather than the quick joy that is going to be gone in no time. Lagom is meant to help you learn how to build a good life, rather than a life that seems empty and that has you searching for the next high.

How many times have you gone through life and found that you thought one thing, or another, would make you happier, but after the initial happiness, you found that it was not enough for you? The disappointment cycles, hitting you again and again. However, when you work with lagom, you are going to focus more on a type of contentment, and this is going to ensure that you can increase your levels of happiness. Moreover, who wouldn't want to increase the amount of happiness in their own lives?

You Will Become Healthier

Living in excess or in deprivation is never considered to be a healthy way to go about your life. Your mind and your body are not going to do that well when it comes to either extreme in the long term. By practicing lagom, you are going to help in maintaining some of your internal stability and will ensure that the mind and the body will be kept in homeostasis.

With lagom, you are going to learn how to do more of the healthy things that you need with balance. You will learn how to reach the right amount of working out, rather than doing too much and wearing yourself out - or too little, skipping out entirely on the health benefits of exercise. It is possible to have too much of both, so learning how to balance these can be so important.

Another benefit to your health with lagom is the improvement in your mental health. When you apply this kind of moderation to your life, your emotions and your brain are not going to fight against each other, and they will not feel quite as in flux as they may have before. Anxiety is often going to be caused by the individual feeling too overwhelmed on a regular basis. Stress is easily taken away when you add in some more moderation to your life, and almost every part of your body and mind can improve when you reduce your levels of stress.

Truly being able to apply the principles of lagom to your life can be helpful because it is going to ease your life. It allows you to have the permission needed to rest when you need it and know when it is time to work and get things done, as well.

Lagom is a Part of Being Mindful

When we are able to learn how to become more mindful, we are learning how to become more aware of the things around us. It is really as simple as that. To have the kind of moderation that is necessary to work with lagom, we need to be mindful.

Think about some of these following questions. How often do you get up to get a snack and then go back to the couch to watch another episode of your favorite show, just to find out that you have eaten the whole bag? Well, while this is something that all of us have done at some point in our lives, and this is certainly not what we are talking about when it comes to moderation! When we behave this way – eating too much of something like chips or cookies or some other unhealthy sort of snack – it just upsets our stomach, disrupts our usual diet, and leaves us feeling ashamed and defeated.

When we are considering the principles of lagom, we are going to learn how to add in some more moderation to our lives. With moderation, you are going to be more mindful. This is a tricky cycle to learn how to get just right, but it can really help you to reduce the amount of stress in your life, improve your amount of happiness, and make you feel like you have been able to level out your life a little bit.

Of course, we are not just talking about moderation and mindfulness when it comes to food. We want this to expand out to all areas in our lives as well. You need to learn how to be more moderate about your social media intake, your work, your relationships, with the levels of activity that you do, and more. It takes some time to add this into all of the things that you want to improve in your life, but starting with just one area of your life at a time and trying to improve as much as you can one step at a time *can make a difference.*

There are many different ways that you can add more mindfulness in your life, and there is no shortage of various techniques that you are going to be able to reach this mindfulness. Of all the methods and ways to reach a state of lagom in your life, you will find that one of the best ways is to reach that state of moderation and happiness is in this guidebook: mindfulness.

Mindfulness not only reduces some of the bad stress going on in your life, it also helps you appreciate some more of the small things that you already get to enjoy on a regular basis. Too many times, we are overworked and too busy running from one place to another, without any break in between, getting upset that time is passing too quickly. With the lagom idea of life - learning how to slow it down a bit and enjoying our lives becoming more mindful - we can really see and appreciate some of the little things that are there as well.

There Can be A Lot of Fulfillment in "Just Enough"

We live in a culture that is all about getting more and having more. We think that we need to have this thing and that thing. We go into debt to keep up with the neighbors and to have the best and the most of everything. This never makes us feel good for long; we are going to feel overwhelmed and tired and have to work more to pay off the things that we no longer need or even find happiness with. This is the exact idea that lagom works towards fixing in our lives.

To look at this from another angle, we need to be able to look at what lagom really is about. Lagom is partially about fulfillment.

Living a life that is fulfilled is not about having the most for everyone; nor is it about having the least. Fulfillment is really just about finding the things in life that are going to help spark a fire in your soul and living in a way that will continue to help feed that fire.

Moreover, we do not want that fire to be around for a short amount of time and then disappear. We want to make sure that we can take that fire and keep it healthy and strong. To do this, we need to be able to find a nice balance between what you are putting into that fire to keep it going. Lagom is the perfect solution to help you maintain your fire and will help you to get there with less time - and less difficulty - in the long run.

This can a challenging thing to do when we are working within the modern American lifestyle. Americans seem to be all about more consumption, having more, and always going for more. However, this "more" is not what is making us happy at all. In fact, it is making us miserable, making it very difficult to ever relax, have free time, or even finding time to hang out with our friends and other loved ones in our lives.

A nice thing to consider: lagom and the way that encompasses the Swedish lifestyle could be the one thing that has it all figured out. It can help strike that balance between what our energies are being used for, without hitting extremes on either side. Life in moderation is one of the best ways for anyone to live, regardless of where they live, what they do, or what their interests are. Between the benefits that come with your physical and mental health – plus the mindset shifts that are going to be created by living a simpler and more moderate existence, lagom is going to be just right for your life.

With the belief in Sweden that everyone should have enough, but not too much, this could be one of the biggest reasons why Sweden, rather than America, is consistently rated as one of the happiest and best places to live. And it is mostly from this principle that we have already been discussing in this guidebook. While it may be hard to get started with moderation in the beginning (especially in the consumerist society that is so popular right now), we will see that making these changes and switching our mindset can be the trick that we need to live a much better life, one that is happier, better, and so much more worth living.

Lagom may be a process that seems somewhat foreign and new to a lot of us who are not from the country of Sweden, but it might be exactly what a lot of us are going to look for in order to improve our lives and find more happiness overall. It may take some shifting of your mindset and your way of living, but it is not as drastic and life changing as some of the other types of options that you can go with. That is one of the best outcomes that results from implementing lagom in your life.

Chapter 3: Adding Lagom into Your Home Life

The first place we are going to ta look in order to help you to really make sure that lagom is added into your life is in your home. You spend a good deal of your time in your home. You sleep there, enjoy time with your family, eat and cook there, take in some peaceful time, entertain, and feel safe and comfortable while you are in that area. It makes sense that you will want to spend some time adding in some more lagom into your life and you will want to start with this process in your own home.

There are a few different steps that you can begin taking in order to add in some more of the lagom principles into your own home. Of course, we need to make sure that we are going with "just enough" as the idea, and this can fall over into your decorating, and even the style that is present in your home. Remember that everyone is different, and this lifestyle is not going to ask you to conform to something that makes you act just like everyone else. Each person who adopts lagom is going to find that it can provide them with some good balance than they may not have had before, but they can still add their own twists to the mix.

To start, we need to take a look at some of the different décor tips, as well as some other tips that work well with the lagom principles. Some of the things that you can do to add more lagom into your home include:

Declutter the Home

To start with, decluttering your home can help to add in more of the lagom as well. A simple and balanced home is one of the best ways for you to achieve a lifestyle that is considered lagom. Not only does a lot of excessive décor all over the place start to contribute to the amount of anxiety that you feel (which can be bad for all parts of the body and mind), it is also going to block out some of your creativity, and can make it almost impossible for you and others in the home to relax.

The good news is that it is easy to declutter the home, and it is possible to do this without having to pay someone or spend a lot of money getting started on this. Start out by practicing lagom with the advice of "one in, one out" rule. This means that for each time that you buy and bring into the home, one item needs to go out. By practicing some small tasks on a regular basis, you will find that decluttering your home is going to be more manageable than ever before.

Choose White or Gray

If you are looking to get started with a new painting project in your home, then changing the walls to gray or white is the best choice for you. Both shades are good for brightening up space and can allow for accent pieces and any other items that you choose for that room to start standing out. In addition, the color palette is muted can really turn the home into a haven that is more relaxing to escape to after you finish up at work – or after completing all of the other obligations that you have during the day.

Of course, this does not mean that you are going to be stuck with just white and gray all of the time and that lagom isn't going to allow for other colors throughout the décor that you have. Instead, you should make it your main focus to create a sense of calm by avoiding brash or loud colors and patterns whenever it is possible in your home.

Bring Some More Nature Into Your Home

It is possible - and often encouraged - to use nature as a kind of accessory in your home. You can use a wooden table or use plants to help work with your decorations as well. Those lagom principles are going to lend themselves closer to minimalism than anything else, being able to introduce some nature into your home can be one of the best ways to brighten up space without trying to add in some more clutter. You can just add in some texture as well with a stone table or going further in any manner that you want, or just go through the process of introducing plants into your home.

Just having one plant in your home is a great way to help reduce how stressed out you feel. Even if there are not a lot of sunny windows in your home to support a plant, some great plant options that you can use are not going to require the same kind of upkeep as others. Options that you can choose to add into your home to follow this principle of lagom and to make sure that you are using plants that thrive with even a a limited amount of sunlight includes Madagascar dragon trees, leaf fig trees, spider plants, and aloe vera plants.

Let in some of that natural light

Given the fact that Sweden has a lot of long winter nights, the décor that comes with lagom is definitely going to focus on getting in as much of that natural light in your home as possible to give you more daylight and to warm the space up. When it is coupled together with a wall that is gray or white and you will find that the natural light is basically going to bounce around your home and can increase your happiness.

To achieve this kind of lighting, you can go with sheer window curtains and windows that are unobscured. These are good ways to make sure that as much of that natural light is able to get into the home as possible. If you are worried about how much privacy that you will have, but you would still like to follow along with this part of lagom, you can look for light and thin drapes that are going to let in some of that natural light that you want. You can also invest in some rolling blackout blinds for the nighttime so you can let that light in during the day and get more sleep at night.

Make sure that the objects in the room are able to breathe

As much as possible, try to set single items so that they apart from one another to give them some breathing space, as well as the spotlight that they really deserve. When you are doing some décor in lagom, each object needs to either serve a purpose or to delight you in some manner. In setting them apart from one another, it allows the room to feel less cluttered and makes it easier for you to appreciate the beauty and the purpose of each piece along the way.

Use some candlelight with a nice warm glow

Candles are going to be something that those who practice lagom are going to use on a regular basis because it helps to add in some of the ambiance to the room that they want. But they take this further than just using the candles in the evening. These candles can be featured at the breakfast table and even around the living room to make that area feel more welcoming and cozier at the same time.

It is important to fill your home with candles in places where you would like to add in a touch of light, such as in the center of the table or a dark corner. Work to balance the space, and make sure that shelves or another location is not going to be cluttered with too many candles in one place. Strive for equilibrium in your use of candles; instead of using too many in one place – or all over the place – set aside your extra candles so you will always have some on hand.

Replacing the carpets with rugs

Rugs are something that will be pretty common when you work on the décor of your home, as carpet is often considered as unhygienic. Transmatta, which translates to the term for "rag rug" in Swedish, will be a typical style that is seen within many homes. These rugs are made from scraps of clothing or old fabrics and are woven together using a loom.

If you are not able to find one of the transmatta, there can be some other simple rug styles of your choosing. To help you to create your own kind of makeshift carpet without dealing with some of the upkeep, layer rugs are going to be on top of each other, and can cover up the floor much like a carpet, but it will help you to take the rugs up and clean them easily whenever it is needed.

Mix together some of the modern and the vintage

Décor that is done in lagom is going to emphasize many things. It is going to mix together the comfortable ergonomic pieces with some of the vintage and stylish ones. This means blending antique pieces with modern ones and slowing down and searching for the best item to suit each space. Vintage furniture and some of the other décor pieces are going to be inherently lagom and in many cases, one person's trash can easily become the treasure of another's.

When searching for some of the décor and vintage furniture that you want to work with, make sure to have some patience. Measure out the space that you would like to fill, and then make sure that you are flexible in the process. You could go into a store and be imagining that you want one piece in your head, and then find that you run across something that is much better instead.

There are a lot of things that you can do in your lagom home in order to make it more comfortable and to ensure that it is going to be "just enough" to make you happy. Follow some of these tips to help you clear up your home and get it all comfortable and ready to go, and you will be well on your way to implementing more of the lagom philosophy in your own life.

Chapter 4: Adding lagom into Your Work or Office

The next place where we can add in a bit of lagom to our lifestyle is in the office. The Swedes do not just implement the idea of lagom only at home, they try to implement it into many different parts of their lives, ensuring that they can have that happiness in many different places, not just one. A collaborate approach and a work-life balance that is healthy is part of the Swedish mindset with work can even help a business benefit if they are willing to use the ideas of lagom as well.

Any employer who would like to create a place of work that is innovative and collaborative amongst all of the employees could really take some tips from the Swedish idea of lagom. The idea of "just the right amount" means that we need to favor things like collectiveness, balance, and moderation over hierarchy, overwork, and individualism. It may be quite a bit different than what we are going to see in an American culture, but it is still an appealing proposition to work with.

Being able to achieve a sensible balance between work and life for all employees is going to be important for any business, whether they are in Sweden, in America, or in many of the other countries on this planet. In addition, the 80-hour workweek is going to be unheard of when it comes to lagom; this long workweek would be counterproductive when trying to assimilate the ideas and processes that are embraced by lagom in your life. Working 80 hours a week or more may make you a lot of money, but between that and sleep you are not going to have time for family, friends, or even relaxation - all important in lagom as well.

For example, one Swedish start-up taking place in California avoids any monthly key performance indicators in the workplace. According to Lars Nordwall, the COO for this business, that this kind of target is going to force people to work long hours. As a result, they may cancel some of their own planned time off in order to get those performance numbers higher or to make up for any of the poor planning that may have happened during that time. This may sound good on the outside, but it results in a culture inside the business of mistrust, stress, and a lot of lack of motivation.

Instead, they like to follow what is known as an "annual operations plan", and the staff members there are included in the formation of this plan. We assume that people will work 40 to 50 hours a week, and that is it. The managers are coached and expected to refrain from asking for more from their employees; this is so that the staff does not experience a burn-out. This is done by making sure the managers, as well as the staff, plan ahead on things to ensure that they prioritize their workdays in a better way. This company even encourages the employees to take time off and leave the workday early on occasion.

The idea here is that the employees need to feel trusted. They do not need to be micromanaged all of the time, having someone overhead, monitoring them all every moment of every day, making them work 60 hours a week, and never allowing them to have a home life at all. This may make sense to the business owner who gets to take home a lot of money in the process, but it discourages employees, making them feel overrun and tired in the process, and this is never good for any employee - or for the company either. When an employee feels like they can be trusted, it is more likely that they are going to go above and beyond at any of the times that the business is going to need it more.

Think about it this way: if you are already working 60 hours or more a week, do you really want to add on more hours and more stress to take care of a business that is only interested in dollar signs and working you even harder? Or, would you put in more work and effort if you knew the business is valued you, letting you work just the 40 hours without guilt, gave you time to leave early if you had an appointment or wanted to take care of the kids, and didn't try to overwork you all of the time?

Another example of this is from Lars Bjork, an owner of a software business in Pennsylvania. According to Bjork, the only way to strike the right balance between work and home is to test and see what works, "swinging the pendulum," as he likes to put it. In this business, the staff has the option to work from their own homes instead of coming into the office all the time, and then they are allowed to experiment with their choice. The employees need to come in on occasion for some client meetings, but otherwise, they are allowed to work at home to help make things easier and to maintain a better work to life balance.

Another part of the lagom process that is found in the office is teamwork. This is why many companies created on this important principle are going to make decisions in a more collaborative manner. Employees are able to use various processes or attend meetings so that they are informed and can speak up on the process of making decisions for the whole company.

When an employee is able to make some of the decisions that affect the company, it is going to be really great for everyone. They know why certain things are going to be put into place, they can talk about the problems they see and try to make it better, and they can really work to feel less stress. They will feel like their opinions matter, even if they did not vote for all of the decisions that were accepted. In addition, because of their involvement in decision-making, the employees will feel less stressed out. Instances of mistrust, misunderstandings, and disputes are going to become much rarer compared to many American companies.

The goal with this overall idea is to come up with a consensus. Not everyone is going to be happy with all of the decisions all of the time, but the point is to strive for a consensus and as soon as the leader of that company or the group makes a decision, it is important that everyone in the business respects the decision and sticks with it. While the employees are asked to speak up and let their thoughts and opinions be known, it is also made clear in these kinds of businesses that the leaders get to come in and make the final decisions.

Therefore, with these is in mind, there are going to be a few different things that need to show up in a company and in your work life to make sure that you are adding in some of the lagom processes into it will include:

• Keep the work weeks to a minimum. When it comes to lagom, the 60 hours or more a week idea needs to disappear. No one is benefiting from this. It is simply resulting in employees who are worn out and tired, and who aren't performing as well as they should. Limiting the hours to 40 hours will be plenty for most companies and can result in employees who are more willing to go above and beyond when the time calls for it with their employer later on.

• Allow for some time to work at home. Sometimes, life comes up, and employees are going to need to be at home with a child, with their spouse, or because their car broke down. Forcing them to take days off and miss out on paychecks because of these life events can add to a level of stress that is not going to be good for them, or for your business. They miss out on money they need for bills, and you miss out on some of the productivity that is needed.

• Some businesses have started becoming more open in terms of the amount of time they allow their employees to work at home. This isn't possible for every business all the time and, of course, you may have to outline times when the employee needs to make it into work. That said, allowing some flexibility can ease the stress that your employees have, and can help you to still get the work done that you need.

• Do not have metrics that add in too much stress. Too many American companies spend their time coming up with hard metrics that they expect everyone to meet all of the time. They assume that with these metrics, they are going to be more productive and get things done. However, these just add in a lot of stress to your employees as they try to keep up, working harder and harder to meet the metrics.

• Instead, allowing the employees to have some say in the planning and in the metrics that are used can make a big difference. This will ensure that they can bring up some of their own concerns with the metrics that are being used and can help to ensure that the things that are being done are actually going to improve your business. You may be surprised by how much work can be done when you are not stressing employees out as much in the process.

• Allow for a safe and open environment for everyone. Everyone in the company needs to feel like they are valuable. Making them feel like they are only there to make the company money, and making it a big deal when they have to take time off, when they ask a question, or when they make a valid opinion, can really be detrimental to the employee, and to your business. Your business cannot run without the employees, so why treat them as if they should be machines that have no opinions or private life outside of the workplace.

• Consider listening to all employees when making decisions. Instead of having just one person in the business in charge of all the decisions (stepping on the toes of everyone else), why not consider having everyone involved make some of the decisions as well? Sure, it is fine to have one leader who can work to make the final decision, especially if there is not a consensus all of the time. However, when the individual employees are allowed to speak up and feel as if they are heard, it is much easier to make them feel as if they are a valuable part of a team, rather than just a number.

• Realize that your employees have - and want to have - a life outside of work. Employees like to go home and not have to worry about work. They want to have more time to go out, see friends, visit family, and spend time with their spouse and their kids. They do not like to have their employer calling them all of the time about an "emergency" that takes up hours of their life. In addition, they do not want to spend 60 hours a week at work and then spend more time on the weekends and at night trying to get more work done. They want to have the freedom to go home, turn off from work, and do the things that they like.

If you are trying to add more lagom into your life, this is the kind of job that you need to look for. Even if it may not be the highest paying job, finding one that allows you to take a breather, and not have to think about and do work all of the time, rather than the things that you want to do, can really help to improve your life and make it so much better overall.

In the American culture, most people struggle with the many issues of balancing a good work life with the rest of life. Many companies think that the best way to be productive and to get things done is to overwork employees, trying to get the very most of from worker. In the process of caring only about productivity, they have a high turnover or employees who are not motivated to do the job; this is harmful to the overall business.

Adding in some of the ideas that come with lagom can be one of the best ways to fix this issue. Including more freedom, reducing (or ending) all stopping all of the micromanaging, and cutting down on the long work hours can be the best way to have employees who are happy. There will still be plenty of – and likely more - productivity with the employees as well. Following the tips in this chapter will ensure that you are going to be able to see the best results with your employees.

Chapter 5: Lagom and Your Clothes and Wardrobe

The next part of lagom that we need to consider is how to handle your wardrobe and the clothes that you wear when following the principles of a lagom lifestyle. This includes learning how to keep your clothing and your wardrobe to a minimum so that you do not feel overwhelmed. Trying to keep up with all the costs of buying new clothes, as well as the expense of washing them all of the time, can be stressful. Now, we are going to spend some time looking at how you can make your entire wardrobe conform to the ideas of the lagom lifestyle, saving you a lot of time and money in the process.

The basis of a lagom closet is keeping the number of items down to a minimum; you do not need many items in your lagom closet. If you can barely get the closet door to open at all, then this is a sign that you are not living lagom at all! You want to have clothes that can be reused and changed up easily, clothes that are going to last, and ones that may work for formal and informal occasions depending on your needs. It is not unusual for the people of Sweden to go with just a few items of clothing and then mix and match them to get the looks that they want.

This can sometimes sound boring. You may worry that people will start to notice that you are wearing the same things all the time. However, in reality, no one is really going to notice at all, and it is going to save you a lot of time and money. When you do not have to spend hours looking for the right outfit or trying to find something, and when you do not have to spend all that time washing your clothes, you can have the freedom to do other things. In addition, when you only need to purchase a few items to start with, it can really save you a lot of money as well.

There are a few things that you can consider working with when it comes to adding some lagom into your lifestyle. First, see if you can give your wardrobe a kind of facelift. As the fashion scene starts to move on and some of your styles goes with it, the way that you look at your clothes is going to change. Make sure that you go through your wardrobe on a regular basis, without making the focus passing things on.

You may be surprised at what is in the wardrobe, and what you would be able to wear again in a different manner. Maybe you find that you have an old skirt and see that it can now work perfectly as a quirky petticoat for an old dress that needs a lift. Maybe you can find some pants that you can rework into shorts and make them last a little bit longer.

The next thing to consider is dusting off that sewing machine. This is a great skill to learn; sewing can help you to keep some of your clothes for a bit longer and save money in the process. Maybe you start out by learning how to sew a button back onto a shirt, then you learn how to work with zippers, and possibly even learn how to adapt one of your own garments into something that is brand new. Consider watching some YouTube videos, and look into other similar learning options that can help make this a reality.

You also need to take some time to evaluate the capsule wardrobe that you have. Having a base of clothes that are useful (and that you enjoy wearing) can be great, but we need to consider this idea carefully; you may have a different idea of a capsule wardrobe than someone else. Maybe you have a base that has 11 floral-based dresses, while someone else wants to have a reliable range of trainers and waxed coats.

The next thing to work on is bravery: try out some of the matches which might seem ugly to you at first. It is something that may be hard to get started with, but it is really liberating to someone when you try something new out, get it wrong, and then just learn how to live with it. It is only by doing experiments that you are able to learn more about your own personal expressions, and you can become better at trusting your instincts when it comes to your style. Who knows, you may find that you fall in love with something that doesn't exactly fit the current trends? It's a learning experience.

There are also a few things that you can do to make your wardrobe more functional. Wardrobe changes will ensure that you have the outfits that you need, without all of the extras or unneeded pieces still hanging in your closet, taking up room. Some suggestions include:

1. Take good care of your clothes. Buying good quality helps your wardrobe to survive the rain and the cold, and even some of the hotter temperatures. Think about the long term with your clothes and get stuff that is higher in quality and will last longer – then take care of them! Yes, it may be more expensive, but if you can pick out a coat or a pair of pants that lasts for five or more years, rather than just one season, it is going to be much more advantageous for your wallet.

2. Forget what is going on with trends. When you follow lagom, and you go for the long term, you have to forget about the fads because these are short term and are going to change all of the time. Pick the style that you like, and then stick with this.

3. Put some of your comforts first. Nothing is going to ruin your day than going with shoes that barely fit or are not comfortable. You want to make sure that all of the items that you wear and put on your

body are not just functional, but also comfortable so that you can make sure you are enjoying life more.

Changing up your wardrobe a bit when you are trying to follow lagom is sometimes hard. It is difficult to think about the long term when picking out the clothes that we want to wear, and sometimes it is easier to follow the trends knowing that we can change out of this all the time. However, with lagom, we think about comfort, we think about the long term, and we find items that are going to last us and will stick around and last us.

This is hard to manage sometimes, but it is going to be necessary to ensure that we are going to save money and have just enough. You may have to limit yourself on going out and purchasing something new all the time. Moreover, you may have to say no to things more than you would like. Nevertheless, the reward that comes with this is going to be so worth it in the long term and can bring you more happiness than ever before.

Chapter 6: Lagom and Your Food and Eating Choices

Lagom is something that you are able to work with when it comes to your eating choices. The American way of eating is not something that the rest of the world is going to share. Most countries are going to practice some more moderation when it comes to the amounts and types of foods that they eat. It seems in America that there is a lot of extreme; either people eat excessively and bring ruin to their health, or they eat so little that it can cause physical issues as well. However, with the idea of "just enough" that comes with lagom, we would be able to fix this kind of problem and learn to enjoy our food while maintaining our own health in the process.

When it comes to how you should eat, and eating well, lagom means that you should find balance; this means having an awareness of what your body actually needs, learning how to find your cues of satisfaction, and gauging how you feel as you are eating. This keeps things healthier and moving along better than eating until you are stuffed or only eating because it is time to eat, rather than what we think we should eat or whatever is on the plate.

The Swedes are often all about everything being in the right amount, but this does not mean that they are going to be afraid to treat themselves at times either. One only needs to take a look at all of the candy bins that are on the walls of all the stores in Sweden to see this. However, those who live in this country have a system for the treats, and they know when to treat themselves, and when to eat in a healthier manner.

For example, "lordagsgodis", which means "Saturday candy", is a tradition that has been around Sweden since the 1950's. The Swedish government (worried about the problem of dental caries in the country) recommended to parents that they give candy to their children only on Saturdays. To this day, if you are out shopping on a Saturday, you are going to see children out filling paper bags with gummy candies and licorice, even the kind that is saltier.

This can be a nice way to include a treat in your life. You do not have to completely give it up, but you learn how to limit it as much as possible along the way. You get avoid sweets and candies most of the time in order to keep your body healthier overall. Still, you'll have something to look forward to at the end of the week, and you can enjoy it in moderation, without giving it up all of the time.

Another option that you can work with is learning how to plate your foods. The Swedes like to take a more social kind of mealtime than what we are going to see with many American families. When it is time to eat (even at lunchtime in the workplace), they are going to place their food on real plates, and then sit down at a real communal table so that everyone will each lunch together. Sometimes there will be candles that are lit, and the conversation is going to include everyone rather than just one or two people talking to each other.

Unlike what many Americans are going to do during lunch, hardly anyone is going to eat out of a Tupperware container! You will not eat alone at your office; you will not go out to eat for lunch. You will not eat with just one other person and feel alone the whole time. In addition, you will not have to work during your mealtime either.

This is all about working with others and having a break when it is time. Eating a meal that is plated makes it more formal and more of an event, and when you can actually leave your work behind to sit and talk with others at the table, it makes the experience so much better.

This is not just in the workplace, though. Those at home make sure that their meals are done on a plate as well. And even those at school or at a daycare are going to have their lunch plated and they will be seated at a table with a hot lunch, the right kind of cutlery, and a chance during the whole time in order to learn how to behave and use the right kinds of manners at the table as well.

This is something that takes a bit of time to grow accustomed to. Most Americans are used to rushing their lunch, trying to get it done as quickly as possible and not focusing too much on what they are eating (or how much they are eating!) They often eat alone and do not really enjoy their lunch because they know they are not really getting a break, often having to work at the same time, and missing out on the social experience that can come with it.

Once you make some of the changes, you will find that it really can be pleasant. Not only does this kind of eating more social, it is going to add some element of respect to the whole idea of eating - and eating well. Taking the time to plate your lunch on an actual plate and then sitting at a table with others (not at your desk) can turn the process of eating lunch into a more mindful act, allowing you to really enjoy the meal more than eating alone, eating at your desk, or while you are doing some work.

Another thing to learn when it comes to eating with the idea of lagom is that you do not have to fear fat. Letting go of a lot of the myths that are popular in America and eating things that have healthy fats in them can be a hard thing for many Americans who are worried about their diets and how healthy they can be. Still, this is something that you need to move past when it comes to eating in a balanced way on this kind of diet plan.

For example, those in the Swedish country are going to favor dairy that is full of fat, and once you get over the idea that all fats are bad, you will start to see why and enjoy this version over some of the others. But it is not going to end just with the dairy products that you consume though. Swedes enjoy having butter to be full in fat, cream sauces, and they will add in a lot of cheese to their meals – a lot more than you may be used to. This may be a lot different than what we think of as healthy, but it can be good for you if you do this consumption in moderation.

Even with this higher level of fat intake, it does not seem like the Swedes are overeating or gaining a lot of weight. This is because the right kinds of high-fat foods tend to be more satisfying, and good at helping you to not overeat, compared to some of the lower-fat options. If you learn how to listen to some of your own satisfied cues and do not take this too far, you would be able to lose weight and stay healthy the whole time, even when are eating foods that are higher in fat.

In addition to eating foods that are higher in healthy fats, you also need to make sure that there are a variety of grains present in your diet. Of course, there is going to be the regular kinds like rice and wheat, but when it comes to the type that most Swedes like to consume, rye is king in that country.

In Sweden, oats are going to be consumed in savory form, as an alternative to rice that is both more sustainable and more nutritious. Food oats, or Mathaver, are going to be chewier and thicker than some of the flaked or rolled oats that most Americans are used to working with, and it helps to make a better meal. Spelt is another common grain, as well, and can be eaten in many different forms and even baked into bread if you like.

Eating lots of healthy fruits and vegetables can make a lot of difference in the kinds of health that you are going to have as well. Try to add in some variety along with the other two food types that we have discussed. These are going to provide your body with a ton of great antioxidants and nutrients that the body needs and can be a great way for you to really get something sweet without having too much through the week and ruining the kind of moderation that you need.

Lagom is going to help us to slow down and listen to our bodies about how much to eat. If you are eating too quickly, it is hard to know when you are done with eating, and when you have had too much. Remember that lagom is all about *just enough*, so you should eat just enough to make the stomach happy and provide your body with the nutrients that it needs, and nothing more. But how are you supposed to know when you reach that point in eating if you have not slowed down enough to feel it?

Lagom is going to help us to actually enjoy our meals. Instead of going through and just scarfing down the food that you have all the time, without really tasting it or even remembering what you ate from one meal to the next, lagom asks you to slow down and actually get a chance to eat your meal and really enjoy it. This is so important for anyone who is trying to be healthier overall, and it can really make the whole idea of eating more enjoyable.

Slowing down, tasting the food that you eat on a daily basis, and being more mindful will make a big difference. You will enjoy the food that you are eating. You will slow down quite a bit and enjoy the mealtime as well. In addition, you will find that when you are able to slow down a bit, you can actually tell when you are satisfied, rather than overeating and then feeling – when it is too late - that it is time to stop.

Lagom is going to ensure that we eat more healthy foods that are better for us. Lagom is definitely not against the occasional treat. However, this does not mean that you should have so many treats that you are not being able to really watch the foods that you are eating along the way. Your diet should consist mostly of healthy foods, with lots of good protein, good whole grains and options, healthy fats, and good fruits and vegetables along the way. If you are able to eat these on a regular basis, you can then have treats on occasion – without the guilt!

Lagom allows us to turn our meals into a more social event, rather than hurrying through them. If you are used to eating alone all of the time, or you are used to eating at a desk while doing work, you probably already know that this is bad for a lot of different reasons. You are alone, which can be a bit depressing and does not allow you to get any socialization in. In addition, since eating at your desk often means that you are going to be working at the same time; this means you are not really getting a break in the process.

No matter what meal you are eating, lagom encourages it to be a social event. Sit down as a family and enjoy the breakfast together before you head off to school and work. Take some time during the workday to sit down with others in the office and talk, without excluding anyone, and be sociable. At night, either eat with your family or invite a friend over to enjoy a meal with you. These meals are not just about feeding the body and getting some nutrition in; they are also about taking a break from your day and improving your mental and emotional health AND becoming more social, all rolled up into one.

Lagom allows our meals to be more mindful. When we learn to focus on what we are eating in our meals we become more mindful of the food we are taking in. Take time to plate some of your meals rather than eating out of Tupperware or out of a bag. This helps the food (think fresh) as well as helping us to stop and enjoy the meals that we eat. Changing this one habit makes it easier to slow down and know when we are full, or when we are eating simply because food is in front of us.

It is important through this process that we learn how to actually listen to our bodies. In America, we see what the time is on the clock, and then assume that it is time for us to eat, whether or not we are actually feeling hungry at the time. When we fill up our plate, the plate is usually very large, and we feel like we need to eat every last bit, and sometimes go back for seconds.

While these things are going to help us to stay on a schedule, they are not going to be very conducive to helping us learn the signs and signals that our bodies are sending out, and it often causes us to eat excessively much. It's easy to see the truth in this concept; look at the rise of obesity and the epidemic that it is causing in America, and we see that this is definitely true.

With lagom though, it is important to learn how to cut out some of these habits, stopping them in their tracks. Eating too much food and filling ourselves past satiety is not a good way to maintain our health, and it is going to throw us off that balance that we are really trying to find in lagom. It may be the way that Americans eat, but most of us can agree that it is not the best way to do things and rushing through mealtime causing more harm than good.

The good news is that there are a few ways that you can change up your eating habits to make them fit in more with the ideas of lagom instead of sticking with the bad eating habits that you already have. To start, go with a smaller plate at mealtimes and do not fill the plate to the rim; this alone can cut hundreds of calories and will make you feel full when you are done.

While you are eating, take small bites and actually savor the food. This is where the idea of mindfulness is going to come into the picture and make things easier. After every two or three bites, take a drink of water as well. This helps to slow down your eating and keeps you hydrated so that you will not speed through the eating so fast. Often, we miss out on our cues of being satisfied because we are eating so fast, the stomach gets filled up before we can even realize what is going on. When we slow down, we can tell when we feel satisfied, and this is often going to be earlier than we even realize.

After you are done eating, do not go back for seconds. Your first plate is often going to be enough, and unless your stomach is still growling and begging for food, which is most likely isn't (so don't use this as an excuse,) you do not need to head back to get more food. Stick with the one plate and you are going to feel so much better.

When it comes to your mealtimes, mix things up as well. Just because you have gotten out of bed, or because it is noon does not mean that you have to eat at this time. This is what many Americans are conditioned for, but it is an unhealthy way to eat. It makes us feel like we need to eat at that time, even if we are not really feeling hungry. Learn how to read the hunger cues of your body and listen to those cues to tell you when it is time to eat, rather than the time on the clock. Depending on your own body, you may find that you do not need to eat as often as you thought in the past.

The idea of lagom is going to come into play many different ways when it comes to the way that you eat. It asks us to slow down a bit more so that we have a chance to really eat what we need, and nothing more. It asks us to have a chance to enjoy a meal with someone else, rather than always eating too much on our own. In addition, it asks us to enjoy some of the treats and the snacks that we want, as long as it is done in moderation.

This can be in stark contrast to what we are usually see with many of the eating habits in America. Nevertheless, when it is implemented in the proper manner, and we learn how to listen to our own bodies, rather than just eating because we think we need to, then we can see why lagom is such a good process for our whole health.

Chapter 7: How Your Holidays and Celebrations Can Be Improved with Lagom

No matter how much you like Christmas and all of the holiday spirit that comes with it, it is easy to admit that it has been taken over by commercialism – in other words: buying lots of stuff! Millions of Americans go into so much debt in order to really celebrate Christmas and all that comes with it, and this leads to many problems down the line.

The first issue is how much is spent on presents. There is a whole weekend, Black Friday and the days after it, that is devoted to big deals on Christmas presents, and trees are often filled to the brim with lots of different items for everyone in the family. Presents need to be bought for every person in the family, and even for some friends and coworkers and teachers and everyone else. It can cost a small fortune buying all of these presents, and many times even with all of the money spent, these presents will be forgotten about, broken, or in the way in just a few weeks.

The presents are not the only thing to be concerned about when it comes to the hassle with Christmas though. How much is spent on the lights around the house? How much is spent on a tree or on decorating the house, on all those Christmas parties, and all of the other festivities that come around this time? And how much time and money are spent to get all that food cooked and prepared to go see family and friends?

It is not that we do not enjoy these kinds of things, but it all sounds pretty exhausting, too. By the time the holiday is over, we all need a vacation from it, and our bank accounts are so drained that it takes most of the year in order to fix it and try to get things back in line. There has to be a better way to enjoy the good stuff of the holiday, without having such a mess to deal with along the way.

The good news is here that there are some other things that you can do in order to add more lagom into your holidays as well. Adding this into your holidays may seem like you are a bit of a Grinch, but if it helps to maintain your sanity along the way, takes away some of the stress, and helps you to keep to some of your budgets from being busted, then it is definitely something that is worth your time.

So, with this in mind, and remembering that we want to spend more of our time enjoying what is allowed in this holiday, rather than having to stress out and worry the whole time, we need to take some time to look at the different ways that you are able to add in more lagom into your Christmas and the other holidays that are in your life as well.

Christmas cards

There are a few different steps that you can take to handle these Christmas cards. Some people decide that Christmas cards have to be sent out to everyone in their family, and their friends and coworkers and other people they have not seen or talked to in years. They will make or find the best cards, send out hundreds of cards, take family pictures, get stamps, and so much more.

This can be stressful, especially when you stop to consider that people are not going to do anything with them once the holiday is over. This could definitely be a part of the process that you would keep out of your holiday time. It may seem like a hard thing to let go of, but when you don't need to worry about the stress of not getting a card to everyone, or about the cost and time that goes with each one, think about how much it is going to free you up and give you some time to enjoy the holidays!

The Christmas Decorations

The next thing that you can focus on in order to help out with the holiday season is with the decorations that you use during this time. If you really want to go with lagom, you would choose to not really have many kinds of decorations up at all, or just the minimal, like a tree and a few lights. However, some people are really into this holiday and enjoy having some more decorations around to celebrate. This is fine, but we need to find some simple and practical methods of doing this to ensure that we can really see the results and not have to go into debt or struggle at the same time.

There are a number of ways that you can make even your Christmas decorations fall into the realm of lagom. One of the best ways to help you can recycle the decorations that you have for this time of year is to pick out a Christmas tree that you are able to replant in the garden when you are done, or one that you are able to reuse year after year. Just make sure that when they are watered and moist the whole time that you keep them inside so that they are going to live until the holiday is over.

However, for those who do not have enough space to deal with planting a tree when the holidays are over, you may need to go with another option. You can purchase a real tree if you would like, but many people who take the lagom path will purchase a fake tree so that they can just reuse the tree from one year to the next. If you do go with one of the real trees, there are many municipalities who will pick up and dispose of the tree in the most ecological manner possible, and that is something that you should consider.

Another thing to consider is that one of the most lagom ways of decorating your home is to get foliage, branches, and even flowers from your own garden to help decorate the home and make it look good for the holiday. You can use any of the extra branches that you don't need from your real tree, or from the trees that you have outside: ivy, holly, and some of the other seasonal plants from outdoors in order to help decorate up the home, make the hearth and the mantle look better and to make the centerpieces that you need for your table.

You can add in other types of decorations if you would like but consider how much it is going to cost and whether you would be able to reuse it as much as possible. If you go with lights, get a high-quality kind that you will be able to use for a few years in a row. Pick out decorations either that can last through the whole winter, or that you can reuse at other parts of the year without a lot of extra work. The more that you are able to reuse things and make them work for the other things that you will need in life, the easier this process will become.

The Wrapping Paper

We are even able to take some of the wrapping paper that we are using and make it work for lagom as well. You may not realize it ahead of time, but it is possible that a lot of the wrapping paper that you try to send to the green bin cannot be recycled, especially if you find that you go with some that have glitter finishes, is metallic, or has plastic on part of the surface.

An idea that is much better for you is using brown paper to make your own wrapping paper. You can recycle this later. Consider adding some tinsel or using some pretty string; use your imagination to help make your own wrapping paper unique and unusual. Doing this adds a personal touch, giving a unique look that you are not able to find with any of the commercial wrapping papers that are out there.

There are a few different ways that you can do this and even save money in the process. You can keep some of the old paper and bags that you get from the grocery stores and use this for your wrapping paper. If you save the old bags and keep them for a bit, then this is the perfect way to wrap presents without having to spend any money in the process.

Alternatively, you can choose to give up the wrapping paper altogether and go with something like a fabric bag to wrap up some of your presents. You can often find a lot of old pieces of fabric at your home or at a thrift shop and can make a bag that you are able to reuse repeatedly.

The Meal

If you are having a meal at your home for the holiday or throwing your own kind of holiday party, then it is likely that the sheer amount of work that you have to put into it is going to seem overwhelming. It can get expensive to spend your time getting plates, decorations, silverware, nice things for the whole process, and to make all of the meals, desserts, and sides that you would need in order to really have a nice party.

You do not have to go through all of this process and feel so stressed out in order to have a nice holiday with some of your friends and family. You just need to know where to cut back and where to work hard to make it nice. First, if you insist on cooking the meal, there are a few options to have. You can cut down on the number of sides and desserts that you are going to cook. Choose just one meat that you are going to cook, instead of three options. Alternatively, even ask others to bring along a side, a condiment, or a drink to help. The more hands who are able to help, the easier it is going to be.

Another option here: if you do not feel comfortable with asking your guests to bring in their own foods and parts of the meal, try having your meal catered. There are a lot of affordable options out there with some unique offerings as well, and this can help to cut out some of the stress, allowing you to enjoy your holidays, while still providing your guests with a good meal.

Many times, those who are throwing these kinds of parties are going to worry about every little detail and hope that it is all perfect. However, in reality, your friends and family are there to have a good time and to see you; they are not going to worry so much about all of the little details. Who really cares if you are using paper plates or real China? Who cares if the plates and the cups and everything else actually matches? Having things a little different and a little less formal can make the party that much more fun.

In addition, here, you need to consider how much you can actually take on when it comes to the holidays. Many people like to hit everything during this time, in the hopes that they will be able to squeeze out everything from the holiday, and that they will not make anyone mad. But before they know it, their holiday is stuffed full of parties, school events, work events, caroling, cooking, and so much that they can't sit back and relax and actually enjoy the holiday that they are in. This means that too much is going on, and it is definitely a sign that some lagom needs to be added in.

Before the holiday is even set to start, it is a good idea to take a step back and actually take a look at what is going to come up, and what is the most important to you. Stuffing one or more social events into each day is not a good idea, and definitely is more than enough for anyone to handle. Sure, you can still accept invitations to things, be social, and enjoy the season. However, your time should not be so packed full that you are stressed out.

During this time, before accepting an invitation, consider whether it is something that you would really like to do and really enjoy. Consider who is throwing the party or get-together, how you would feel if you could miss it without making anyone mad and think about how stressful it might make that day for you. In addition, when all of these factors are considered, you can *then decide* if it is worth your time to go to that outing or not.

Christmas presents

The final thing that we need to take a look at when it comes to adding lagom into your holiday time is with the Christmas presents. When it comes to these, we need to take a step back and consider whether we really need to go all out and buy so much for the year? How many of those items do we actually need? In addition, are some gifts that are actually going to be used on a regular basis by your friends and family and your kids, or is it something that is going to be thrown out and never used again?

Yes, it is always a lovely idea to give and receive gifts, but maybe it is time to really consider the giving that we are doing, and not just give out presents for the sake of it. This ensures that the gifts that we do give are more meaningful, useful. Another advantage to thinking through the idea of present-giving: this helps us avoid just picking out the first item we see, spending too much money, in the process.

The best thing that you can do here is to set a budget with the idea of frugality as the main aim here. You may find that *giving memories rather than things* can be so useful to help you to have a better Christmas, without spending money on a gift that is going to be worthless to the other person in no time at all. You could give out a voucher to do something for the other person or to go somewhere with that other person. Always remember that giving your time is a much better present than any item that you are going to use. You can also consider making a present for the other person as well.

Yes, you will have children who will ask and beg for the latest and greatest thing all of the time. This is nothing new, but it is not something that you need to give into all of the time. You can limit some of the gifts that they get that are just going to be underfoot in no time and work with this instead, giving the experiences and time rather than giving them more things that are going to be in the way again.

Remember here that the idea of lagom is not to get rid of everything, but to make sure that you have just enough when it comes to the different parts of your life. This ensures that you can still enjoy the holiday that is coming your way, rather than stressing out and worrying about all of the different parts of the holiday that make you feel overwhelmed with too much responsibility. This can take some adjustment, especially in light of all of the commercialism that comes with being in America. Still it is one of the best ways to ensure that you are going to be able to really enjoy the holiday and spend it with the people you love, doing some of the things that you really love. And isn't that what we all really want during the holidays?

As you can see, it is possible for you to take the holidays, especially with Christmas, and add in some lagom to it. In fact, once you get over the idea that people are going to judge you or that you are going to miss out on something important during the holiday, this gets easier. You will find that adding in lagom - doing just enough rather than too much during this time of year is - going to make a world of difference in how much you will actually be able to do and enjoy when it comes to the holiday season.

Chapter 8: The Lagom Parenting Style

It is even possible that we are able to take some of the ideas that come with lagom and apply them to your experience and your work as a parent. Parenting is really hard; there are so many opinions and parenting styles that it is hard to know what is going to be the best one for your needs. In addition, it always seems like one person thinks that their style of parenting is going to be better than what someone else is going to have. How do we know when we are parenting in the proper manner, and how can we add the ideas of lagom into the parenting?

Although it is true that parenting is going to be a matter that is very personal, and it is going to vary based on the family dynamics and the children in the family. Many parents are going to decide that it is worth their time to incorporate the lagom beliefs and elements into some of what they are doing when they raise their own children.

Something that may not be that surprising here is that many of these ideas are going to come from the way that families in this country raise their children. Similarly, they may be based on concepts that are becoming really popularized throughout the rest of the world. If you would like to learn more about how lagom can be used in the realm of parenting, and you want to figure out how you can add this into your own home, and into some of the things that you are doing with parenting, there are a few suggestions that you can follow.

Let us start with something simple. You want to make sure that your child is getting enough natural light and natural air as well. This is important no matter what stage your child is in at the time - even as a baby. Whether this means getting them outside to play and enjoy what nature has to offer, or if it means opening up the windows and letting the air in while they play inside and take a nap, then this is what you need to do.

In Sweden, most of the doctors there are going to recommend all of this natural air and light in order to encourage the child to develop a healthy immune system and to feel happier. Of course, if your baby is dealing with some health risks that opening up the windows while napping could aggravate, then, of course, you can avoid this suggestion and go with something else in our list of parenting choices. This is also something that you can discuss with your doctor to figure out if it is right for you and your child.

The next thing that you can add into your parenting style when you are working with the lagom parenting style is that you should spend as much time as you can with your children while also maintaining some balance. Families who live in Sweden make a practice of spending time together often, and they will even be happy to take a long and extended vacation together without it seeming off or out of the ordinary. Parents in Sweden are going to spend a lot of time playing outside with their children and will have a good deal of interest in what is going on in the lives of their children.

This may be quite a bit different than what we are going to see when it comes to an American family. Most of these families are going to spend a lot of time apart because the parents are working. The parents will sometimes go out with the kids, but often the kids are going to be on their own and more independent. This is something that would not be seen when it comes to the lagom lifestyle and the lagom type of parenting.

On the other hand, it is also important for us to keep things as balanced and as in check as possible, and we have to remember that while spending time with our children is important, they are individuals. Children should have their own private time away from their parents and other family members on occasion too. It is important to spend time with them, but respect the boundaries that your children have, depending on their age.

Remember that, in lagom, it is acceptable to work with childcare if it is needed. In Sweden, it is common for the parents to send their children to a childcare facility from an early age, and it is not really something that is going to be frowned upon when you need to get back to work after having a baby. Daycares in Sweden exist in many variations, and there are going to be a lot of options out there for a family to choose from based on what seems to be the best for them.

One thing to remember, though, is that while the daycare is just fine if it is something that works the best for your child, you still need to set aside some time after work and after daycare in order to spend some one-on-one time as a family with your child each day. This helps to keep that bond strong and will make sure that all of the emotional needs of your child are being met, even when you spend the day at work.

For a true lifestyle that is considered lagom, children need to have some encouragement to play outside on a regular basis. Parents also need to make sure that they are getting as involved in this as possible and should either be active with their children when the child is outside, or the parent should remain close by while the children are outside playing.

There are a number of reasons for this suggestion. It can ensure that the child is going to be safe while they are playing and that if something goes wrong, there is going to be someone nearby who will be able to help them out and comfort them. If something goes awry, the parent can fix the issue. Plus, spending time together, especially in the outdoors as much as possible, is going to help the whole family on many levels, including on an emotional level.

When you play outside, get more active, and have a lot of access - or at least as much as possible - to play in the fresh air and in the sunshine, this is going to become a very important part of working with the lagom lifestyle. In Sweden, it is not uncommon for families and their children to play outside, no matter what the weather is doing; families make a point to play whether it is snowing, raining, cold, warm, and everything in between.

As you can see, working with the ideas of lagom parenting are going to be a bit different than what you may be used to when you work with other forms of parenting. It is not really helicopter parenting because it recognizes that the child needs to have some independence and has to be allowed to do things on their own, without a parent on top of them all the time. That being said, it also gives another opportunity for the parent and child to bond, helping to create a close family unit. It is important and it is only going to grow stronger when the family can spend some time together and work to reach a common goal.

This is something that is going to seem a bit strange and hard to comprehend for many American families. It seems like we go between the two extremes in many of the things that we do. A parent is often either on top of their child and being there all of the time, giving the child no time to be an individual. Conversely, American parents go to the other extreme, never being around the child, hardly ever spending time with the child. The idea of lagom parenting is going to help us to find a happy medium that occurs between ends of this spectrum - which can be beneficial to the parents and to the child.

No matter whether you spend time at work, or you get to stay home with your child, it is important that you spend some time as a family unit each day. Go to the park and spend some time playing. Do art projects or some other craft together for some time. Go on longer vacations together and really sit back and enjoy that time that you get to spend together.

By the same token, it is also acceptable – and encouraged – to let your child go free some of the time. If your child wants to set a boundary or is looking to do something that requires them to be alone on occasion, then this is fine. You do not have to be connected at the hip to your child all the time. You just need to let them know that you are always there to love and support them and that you are their biggest fan. Recognizing that they will and do have their own lives - and they want to enjoy this as well - can ensure that they know they have that support, while still being able to grow and develop on their own.

The lagom parenting style is a lot different from what many families in America may be used to at the time they read this. It asks for a good balance to happen between what the family does together, and what the child is able to do on their own. As we discussed earlier, most families in American seem to fall on one end of the spectrum or the other: they are either fine with giving the child all of the independence that they want with no family quality time together, or they will be helicopter parents who never let their children grow and explore and mature on their own.

Finding a happy medium between this can be hard. You want to be able to have that quality bonding time as a family, without a lot of distractions and other things going on, and you want to make sure that your child has a good base to come back to when they need love and support. But you have to also mix this in with your child wanting to be an individual and really get a chance to take off and do his or her own thing. There is no right or wrong answer with this one. But learning what the balance is for your family and for your child is going to make all of the difference.

Just remember, you do need to make sure that whether you are home all day with your child or you work outside of the home and need to send them somewhere else for the day, that it is *your job to actually spend some time with your child.* The amount of time that is necessary is going to vary based on the family, but do not believe that a quick "hi" at the end of the day is going to cut it. It needs to be some high-quality family time - whether that is a taking a walk together, making dinner together, talking, reading, or doing something else that no one else is going to be able to interrupt and get in the middle of.

During the rest of the day, it is fine if the child wants to be a bit independent and do some of the things that they want, on their own. They may want to spend time with their friends; they may want to get into a sport or another kind of activity. Alternatively, they may just want to have some time on their own at the end of the day to pursue their own hobbies and to have some alone time. Allowing for this individualism, along with some open arms for the child to feel loved and supported can be so important as well.

This balance is something that is hard to do and stick with all of the time. But you will find that over time, and with some patience along the way, that this is easier to handle. You and your family have to spend some time figuring out what works best for you. Maybe you and your family like to spend more time together, and only a little bit of time as individuals doing your own things. Alternatively, maybe you like to spend more time doing individualistic things and then coming together at night to share and be a family.

Always remember that the experience of lagom is not going to be the same for everyone who decides to use it. Some people will take a different path than what you may have considered for yourself. This does not mean that their method of using lagom is any better or worse than yours. Adding in some of the lagom parenting tricks and learning how you can really live a happy and fulfilled life with your children can change the way that you view raising your children.

Chapter 9: Lagom in Your Love Life

It is even possible to put some lagom in your love life! This is a place where a lot of people would like to see some improvement, but it is hard to find the right balance when starting a new relationship. You may be busy impressing the other person enough that they are willing to go out with you and start a new relationship; this does not leave you with a lot of time to manage all the other things going on in your life at the same time.

It is a big balancing act to make everything work out the way that you would like, and even when a new relationship is started, you do not want to be stuck in the trap of having one thing take over all of the other aspects. In addition, with the ideas that come with lagom, you will find that you are able to manage this a bit better, giving you a better chance at romance, and a better love relationship overall as well.

Keep the Dates Simple

There are too many people today - thanks to social media and the other aspects that are going on around us - who are trying to compete all of the time. They have to have the biggest dates, get the biggest rings, and do the most daring stunts, just to impress someone and even get started on the date, much less what they need to do for the rest of the relationship.

If all of this already exhausts you, and the thought of having to keep coming up with new and bigger ideas of how to impress others and keep the relationship going, then lagom may be the right thing for you. There is nothing wrong with a grand gesture on occasion, but often the best grand gestures are the small ones that mean the most to you as a couple. When you let go of the idea of all doing all these grand things you think you need to do for other person, just focusing on the two of you as a couple, you will find that it is much easier to have a deeper and a meaningful relationship.

This can go all the way to the kinds of dates that you have as well. While a fancy restaurant can be nice sometimes, having to do the greatest and the best each time is exhausting and expensive. Why not a walk and a picnic, or even just have a nice date night at home with homemade food and a nice movie? This helps to take some of the pressure off both of you and can be a great way to talk and get to know one another.

Remember with lagom that it is going to be all about the balance and how the two of you can create a possible new life together as a couple. In addition, if you start out being out of balance in the first place, it is going to become even harder to gain this balance back later on in the relationship.

Do Things that You Both Enjoy

As you are working on building up a new relationship, it is important that you learn how to do things that both of you enjoy. You do not want to be the only one having fun on all of the dates or the other things that you do! You also do not want to be the one who is bored along the way either. When the two of you do things that you both enjoy, it is much easier to have fun and create a lasting bond that is so good for the relationship.

This may include, at times, going out of your comfort zone and trying something new. Maybe you each take turns picking out the activity and getting the other person to go along with you. However, there still needs to be some balance present to ensure that everyone is getting the attention and getting a chance to do what they want as well. If one person in the relationship is taking over and controlling all of the dates and everything that happens in each one, then there is a big imbalance that is going to show up in that relationship, and a lot of the lagom that you are trying to create in your life, as well as in this relationship, is going to start failing.

Take time out for each other

The next tip concerns the fact that you should take a break from one another and do things on your own on occasion. This tip is going to reveal how it is so important to actually make sure that you are scheduling out time for one another. No relationship is going to grow or flourish if one or both of you are so busy with the other activities in your life that you can never spend time one on one with each other.

This is sometimes hard to do in our modern world, and often it may feel like we are balancing a million plates at once. However, if it is needed, bring out your schedule books and write down a time, just as if you would with any other important meeting. Whether you need to do this once a week or a few times scattered out when it works for you, setting aside some time on the calendar will ensure that you are going to actually see each other.

Your relationship has to fit into the balance with lagom on occasion as well. Even if we do not mean for it to happen, sometimes the other distractions of the world and the other things that we need to take care of on a regular basis are going to bring us down and can make it hard to do this. It is so important for a relationship to grow and flourish by spending time together, so start adding this as something important that needs to happen in your own relationship today to maintain that lagom balance.

Understand that "Alone Time" is Just Fine

When you get into a romantic relationship, it is sometimes easy to let yourself go a bit and want to spend all of your free time with the other person. You want to talk to them all day long, you want to call them, you think about them at work, and you cannot wait to get off and go spend more time with them. While this is something that commonly happens with new love, we have to realize that it is creating an imbalance that is not good for anyone.

Think of how much is being missed out on in the other parts of your life. Your work is likely suffering because all you can do is think about this other person. Your friends and family are getting pushed back and may feel a bit neglected and like they are not as important as this new person is, and they may feel a little left out and abandoned as well. While this is probably not what you had meant to do, it is something that can happen if you are not careful.

This does not mean that spending time with the new love interest in your life is a bad thing. In fact, it is necessary for the relationship to grow and flourish the way that you would like, and for both of you to learn a bit more about one another. However, when it becomes obsessive and includes the two of you only ever spending time with one another, then it is creating an imbalance that is definitely not a part of lagom.

It is perfectly fine to take a break from one another on occasion. Yes, you love each other and enjoy spending time with one another, but there are other things in your life that you need to balance out as well, even when you are married. You need to spend time with your parents and siblings, and maybe even other friends. You may need to go to a work function on your own on occasion. You may want to take some time to do a hobby or just do something on your own and think of how much anticipating you will have when it is finally time for you and your partner to get back together after the short break!

Go at a Speed that is Right for Both of You

Sometimes, we are so caught up in the romance of something that we want to just jump right in and take full advantage of it to move things too quickly. When both parties want to do this and have settled on it being the best course of action for both of them, then this is going to be just fine, and you can move ahead. Remember that the *just enough* can be different for each person, and for each couple as well. Maybe moving faster in the relationship is what works and is just enough for this couple. *Maybe not.*

However, you are bringing two people in the relationship, and while just enough may be fast (or even slow) for one person, it may not be enough (or too much) for the other person. In a relationship, the feelings of both parties must be taken into account. If you are pushing someone to move faster and they do not feel comfortable with it, then this is going to cause some stress and anxiety in the process. In addition, if you are holding someone back, despite their efforts to wait for you and consider you, this can cause some of the same issues in the process as well.

This is why both parties need to be in agreement, and lagom can help. It is very important to spend time talking honestly about what is valuable to you in the relationship and where you are feeling the relationship should go in different stages. In addition, being open-minded to what the other person is saying is going to be critical as well. It is not enough to just say your piece, and then expect the other person to agree. When both parties can be open-minded and pay attention to what the other is saying, they are going to find that it enhances their relationship and makes it stronger. They can work together to find the just enough that is good for both, leaving them able to put the stress behind them and grow and develop a strong and lasting relationship together.

Even the relationships that you have with other people, and in your romantic life, can use the ideas of lagom. You can have a nice time with one another and build up a good courtship with the help of the just enough philosophy, rather than going over the top and having to worry through how to impress them, how much it is costing and more. Moreover, in the long run, it is going to create happier and more lasting relationships overall.

Chapter 10: Can Lagom Save You Money?

It is possible for lagom - when it is used in a proper manner - to even help you to save some money. This may seem a bit strange and may sound like a wild claim. However, when you learn how to live with just enough, rather than with too much and lots of excesses, it is going to result in you being able to make do with less, and that alone will save you money.

The idea of lagom is not to go through your home and throw away everything until you have one pair of clothes and a few dishes to work with. The idea is to just learn how to have a nice balance with things. You can purchase things - but purchase them because they bring you happiness and contentment, rather than because you feel jealous that someone else has them or an advertisement convinced you.

There are a number of ways that the process of lagom is going to be able to help you actually save money, and they are pretty simple. In fact, just by following some of the other tips that we have already spent some time on in this guidebook, you will be able to work with lagom in a manner that helps you to save money. Some of the other methods that you are able to implement into your day-to-day life that will ensure that lagom is being used properly and can help you to save some money include:

Purchase Fewer Things

With lagom, you are going to learn how to purchase fewer things. You do not have to give up on everything that you want to purchase, and you do not have to live your life like a hermit in order to embrace the ideals of lagom. That said, it does require you to learn how to just live with what you need, rather than having a ton of stuff that does not even bring you happiness and ends up just cluttering up your home, making a mess.

It is hard to learn how to live with less in our society. More is seen as better and the more that you have, the more that you can impress others and get them to pay attention to you. This stuff just results in clutter all over the home, and that clutter has been proven to cause anxiety and depression. Just remember having all that stuff means you have to pay for it, maintain it, store it; if you paid with credit, you have big bills and lots of debt to pay off. It is no wonder that you have to work all the time!

That cycle needs to stop. This is in excess, causing us to get out of balance and away from the *just enough* mentality that we should have with lagom. This can be hard, and there are many people – including the marketing team for big companies - that work hard to tell us that we need more stuff. However, we can live with less, and probably be much happier in the process.

Eat Less

The next thing that lagom can help you out with when it comes to saving money is the idea that you are going to eat less. The American diet is full of lots of food, and portions that are not going to be to properly scaled to each consumer's size, or consist of healthy options as they need to be. We spend a large amount of money on the food that we eat; between the grocery store and eating out, the snacks and everything else, it just does not take long before we start to see a lot of our money go down the drain – just for food.

When you decide to live the lagom lifestyle, you learn to eat just enough, rather than too much. This alone is going to save you money because it helps you to learn how to cut out the excess of food that you consume and focus more on just eating what you want. Think of how small your grocery bill is going to go when you can implement this into your own life.

Plus, with lagom, you are less likely to eat out as often, though you can still do this on occasion. However, your goal is more being responsible with your money and doing things in *just enough* fashion. Therefore, the eating out on a regular basis, or all of the time like many Americans, would be out of balance; you need to stop doing this altogether. This could save you quite a bit of money all on its own, especially if you and your family spent a lot of time eating out during the week.

Learn to Spend only on What is Important

One of the best things that you are going to learn when you start implementing lagom into your life is to spend your time and money on ONLY the things that are important. Lagom is a bit different than minimalism, as lagom ideals are not about focusing on getting rid of everything; lagom's focus is living with less. You will certainly try to downsize when you are going through this kind of process, and you learn how to not purchase as much in the future, but the focus is not going down to the bare minimum. It is more about finding a balance between purchasing just to fill a void and purchasing things that will make you happy.

For example, say you are an avid reader. One of your hobbies is reading, and you love to pick out a new book, even if it is from an old bookstore. You enjoy flipping through the pages to see what is there. Perhaps you decide to cut out on some of the other stuff, like eating out, having the latest technology gadget or something else, and spend a little extra on some of the books that you want to read.

Alternatively, maybe you like to travel and make memories with your family. Therefore, you choose to cut out the eating out, and you keep everything to a minimum so that you can afford to travel as much as you want. The trick here is not to deprive yourself all of the time. Finding what is important to you, and what is going to make your life a bit happier, is going to be the key.

No one is going to go through this process in the same manner. You may like books, while someone else likes to travel, and another person likes to paint or listen to music or do something else. You have to do what is important to you. Maybe you want to get serious about your debt, cutting back as much as possible and working to get that debt paid off. *Just enough* is going to be different for everyone. Cutting back on some things, and just spending a little bit on the things that are the most important to you can really do some wonders for helping you to save money - especially on things that were not really that important to you in the first place.

Learn How to Pay Down Your Debts

While we are in this process of embracing the lagom way of life, it is often recommended that you learn how to cut down on some of the debts that you have. The American lifestyle and idea that we need to buy more in order to be happier has certainly put a big dent in our credit, causing us to take on thousands of dollars in debt. This is often seen as the way of life at this time; we are supposed to have debt. We feel that we cannot get a car, a home, a college education, or pay for Christmas without having a credit card and lots of debt to handle it.

The truth is, we can live without the debt and without the credit cards. We simply need to learn how to work with *just enough*, rather than living in excess. Do we need to go to a private four-year university and take four or five years to go to school, or could we go to a public in-state college - or even a technical college - and save money? Can we find ways to keep our car going for a bit longer and save up for a nice car, rather than having to buy the newest car model that just came on the market? Does Christmas need to cost thousands of dollars, or can we do it for a lot less, giving gifts that are more thoughtful and more meaningful?

When you work through lagom with your spending and your budget, you learn that you can easily be happy on less, and you will not have to spend as much money. Moreover, this can give you some extra money to throw at the debt on a regular basis. Before you know it, your *just enough* attitude and way of living has helped to pay off some of the debts you owe, making it easier for you to save up a nice nest egg, do more traveling, and enjoy the life you have even more.

Learn How to Ignore Commercialism

Ignoring the commercialism out there is going to be one of the most important - although one of the most difficult - things that you have to do when it comes to implementing lagom into your life and making sure that you can use this idea to help save some money. This commercialism is all around us. We see commercials and other advertisements saying that we need to get this product or another product in order to feel happy. We see our neighbors and family members purchasing something that may make us feel a bit jealous. We may even see things on social media, like people getting new homes, going on vacation, and more and we feel jealous – leading us to believe that we need to be doing some of the same things as well.

This is a dangerous mindset to get into. These things are not going to make us happy at all and are just going to make it feel like we are always behind. We may get a bit of happiness at the beginning from those items, but it will not take long before that happiness is gone, and we are looking for the next high. Before we know it, we are going to have a house full of stuff, a lot of clutter, and we have to work more and more in order to pay off the debts that we took on for those items.

This is not going to lead to the happiness that we want, and since it is adding in some more stress because of all the extra work that we need to do, we can tell that this idea of consumerism is not going to be the best for our needs. We have to learn how to cut out some of the things that are going to try to draw us back. Whether we learn how to cut down on the social media intake, we turn off the television and not watch all those commercials, put down the magazines, or learn how to fill out a contentment journal (designed to help us to feel happier with the things that we already have in life) we have to learn how to cut out some of that consumerism and live with *just enough*.

Learn Difference Between a "Want" and a "Need"

Another thing that you are able to learn more about when you decide to implement the lagom lifestyle is the idea of a want and a need. These are two different ideas; a need is something like the food you eat and the home you live in. A "want" is everything else, such as the special clothes you want to have, the books, the expensive car, and more.

Lagom is not asking you to get rid of everything that you own and never purchase a single thing. However, it can help you to save money because it allows you to learn what you really need, rather than having you just go out and purchase things because you see it in a commercial, or because a friend has that item, or for some other reason. This can help you so much!

First, it is going to save you money. The less that you go out and purchase the more money you are going to save. When you stop spending money on items that you don't even need, not only will it help you to save some money, but it will ensure that you will be able to decrease the amount of clutter in your home, giving you more peace and happiness in the process as well.

Our consumerist society is not always going to be the easiest to fight against. We are tricked into thinking that many of the purchases we make actually fill our *needs*, when actually they are only "wants." This can make it hard to keep up with all of the different products and purchases that we think we need to have, and this makes life difficult to work with sometimes. However, setting some goals, and remembering the idea of lagom and "just enough" can be a good way to help you be prepared along the way.

It is possible to use lagom to help you to save money, as long as you are willing to fight against some of the commercialism that surrounds us all. It is possible to live a very happy and productive life if we just learn how to live with just enough rather than thinking we need all of the latest and greatest things all of the time. This is hard to do sometimes, especially in a society where more is seen as best. When you are practicing lagom, you can let go of this trap, the trap of purchasing more items, then having to work hard to pay for those items that no longer bring you joy or happiness after a short amount of time, and then doing it all over again. When you use lagom to help you regulate yourself and take in just enough to help you feel happier and more complete, you can definitely save money while also improving your quality of life.

Chapter 11: What About Hobbies That are Considered Lagom?

The next topic that we need to take a look at when we talk about lagom to help improve your life is how it can pertain to your hobbies. While you are taking some time to relax and do the hobbies and other activities that make you happy, it is still important that you can add in some lagom so that you can achieve a good level of balance all in one. You may even decide that you want to take up a few new hobbies that are considered lagom, especially if you feel like something you spend your time with right now is not quite right or is not giving you the happiness that you crave.

We always have to remember as we go through this process that lagom is going to be all about finding a balance. Whether this balance is in our work life or with our family and friends - and even with our hobbies - it is so important to add this to our lives as much as possible. Finding the best kind of balance that we can between work, time with our friends and family, and time to spend doing something we love is so important. Our hobbies are going to be such an important part of all of this!

No matter what you like to do as a hobby, it is important for you to make sure you keep things in balance each time that you try to enjoy that hobby. It is tempting sometimes to spend all of your free time on the hobby, but this is not a good thing for you either. It is better to choose a variety of activities to help you create a true amount of balance in your life. You also do not want to take it so far that you focus on work and nothing else, neglecting to give yourself plenty of time to enjoy all of those hobbies that you love.

If you can, you should consider bringing others into the hobby that you love. You can encourage them to do the hobby with you, do some new hobbies with them to learn something you may not have considered before, or even just show them what you have been working on. When you can share in a hobby with another person, you are able to balance doing your hobby with spending time with those you appreciate and love. This is a fantastic way to add in some more lagom to your life.

Another thing to consider here is that your work should never get to the point of becoming your hobby. Many people, especially those who own their business or who work from home, have a hard time separating our work and the hobby, and sometimes these are going to turn into the same thing. This may be tempting and easy to do, but there need to draw some distinct lines when it comes to what your work is, and what your hobbies are.

A hobby is something that you actually enjoy doing, something that gives you a lot of joy and happiness, not something that is going to bring you a lot of stress. If you take the time to do your hobby and you feel stressed out by doing it - or while doing it - then maybe this is not the right hobby for you to do. It is time, when the stress hits you, to take a step back and look at another kind of hobby that you can do while you emotionally process the source of the issue.

You will find that this process of separating yourself from the stress and emotional issues that come with your hobbies, is actually showing you that your hobbies are inadvertently becoming your *job*. This is why is it is so important to separate these two from each other. You need to have a good amount of balance between the different parts of your life and focusing on having the hobby and your work as the same thing is not going to achieve this balance at all.

Of course, we need to always remember that when we are picking out the hobbies that we are going to insert into this part of our lives, we need to have some of the relaxation hobbies included into the mix. You may be interested in doing some options that are different from this, but if you work with one of the old familiar hobbies, you may find that this not only brings you enjoyment but also helps you to relax a bit in the process.

For example, if you enjoy building things, you can try some woodworking. You can take up drawing or painting if you feel like you want to be creative. Alternatively, you can opt for something like crochet, sewing, or knitting if you would like to have a hobby that is fun and easy to bring along with you anywhere. Sometimes these seem like the old-fashioned and boring choices to make, but when they come to the lagom lifestyle of balance and adding in some relaxation to your life, they are great choices to make.

The good news here is that you can to have complete control over what you add to your lifestyle and what kinds of hobbies you enjoy. If none of the above suggestions sound like they are going to work well for you (or you cannot get into them), then do not stress out. Pick out a hobby that works for you. The goal here is to do something that you love, something that brings you some enjoyment and does not stress you out in the process. If you are able to do this, then any hobby that you choose is going to be just fine.

As you are picking out the kind of hobby that you want to work with, remember that you need to remain frugal. It is so easy to overspend when starting out on a new hobby! The whole point of working on this hobby is to bring yourself some enjoyment and to maintain the *just enough* philosophy as well. You do not want to go into a lot of debt in order to get started with the new hobby or to restart one of the hobbies that you are already doing. If you are worried about balancing your budget and making a new hobby fit in because it costs thousands of dollars or more, then this is going to add stress into your life and will not be the best option for a lagom lifestyle.

It is fine to spend a little bit of money on the hobby to get started, but keep this to a minimum, and be thoughtful and careful about how much you are spending. You do not want any unwanted in your life, so it is going to be imperative that you carefully consider the expenditures involved with your hobby. This is part of the lagom way of life, and your hobbies have to be held to the same standard as the other parts of your life, as discussed in this guidebook.

Remember that lagom is all about balance and *just enough*. Your hobby needs to bring you happiness, peace, and relaxation as much as possible. Spending a lot of money on the hobby and stressing out about how much it is going to cost you will not help you to reach the amount of happiness and fulfillment that you are looking for. It is just as bad as picking out a hobby that is not enjoyable or right for your needs.

Yes, it is possible that you will enjoy and pick out a hobby that is more pricey, such as collecting classic cars, but you still need to take the time to find ways to limit the costs, and create a budget and stick with it when you make any purchase. This is part of your new lagom life. You do not want to go into a large amount of debt for your hobby and then have to go through and work more and throw all of the other aspects of your life out of balance just for this one part.

For example, maybe you set aside a little bit of your income each month in order to purchase the supplies that you want for this hobby. Alternatively, maybe you decide that you do not really need to have all of the hobby-related items that go with it. You can get along nicely with some of the most basic items and be good to go. If you feel that you need one of the items for the hobby, consider writing it down, and then waiting a week or two. Then come back to that list and see how you feel about buying the item or items. You may be able to cross a few items off the list, realizing that they are not that important, and you do not really need them in order to work on that hobby.

Don't stress too much about this part either: Remember that you do not want to have this hobby stress you out because of it not being fun or the costs taking too much of your income. Focusing on something that you enjoy, and something that can take you away from some of the worries and stress that come from work and other aspects of your life can be very important to add in the balance that lagom requires.

There are so many hobbies that you can choose to add to your lifestyle and enjoy, that it makes sense to add them into your life and actually take some time for yourself. This may seem strange or unusual in the American culture but taking time for yourself is not a selfish action. Doing this can actually help you to improve some of the other relationships that you may encounter. Take some time to discover what your hobbies are all about and see how great this can be for your own life and adding in lagom as well.

Lagom can reach into all of the different aspects that come with your life, and this is going to include the hobbies that you want to work with. Picking out hobbies that bring you lots of joy - and even ones that can be done with others you know and love - can be so important to helping you to fulfill your life, reduce the stress, and add in more happiness than you may be able to get from your work life or other areas. While taking some time for yourself can seem selfish and hard to handle in the American culture, it is actually really good for you. By following some of the tips and suggestions in this guidebook, you will be able to enjoy your hobbies in the lagom way.

Chapter 12: Can I Add Lagom Into My Life with Pets?

Having a pet in your family can be a great experience. Whether you have had this family addition for a long time, or this is an animal you have just introduced into the family, a pet can bring a lot of fun, a lot of love, a lot of happiness, and even a lot of peace. Moreover, having a pet can certainly be a part of the lagom lifestyle if you choose. When considering your pet, make smart decisions about how you are going to handle the pet, the stuff you get for the pet, how and what you will feed it, those costs, as well as other considerations. Whether your pet is a dog, a cat, a fish or some other family friend, the suggestions in this chapter will make sure that you get the full enjoyment that you can out of this family friend, while still living the lagom lifestyle on a daily basis.

Even when it comes to your furry (or scaly or feathery) member of your family, it is possible to add in some of the ideas that come with lagom. Pets tend to bring in a lot of joy rather than not, but they are also able to bring in some stress to your life on occasion as well. Keep this in mind while you check out some of the suggestions that we are going to discuss through this chapter so that you can learn the best methods of incorporating lagom into the way that you treat and keep your pets

Just like with some of the ideas that we talked about with parenting earlier on, you are able to create a nice balance in your life; consider this for your pets as well. The proper way that you should discipline and train a pet may be difficult for everyone to agree on, but for many cases, it is best to practice rewarding good behavior in your furry friends. Getting into this kind of habit right from the beginning, when you first bring the pet home, can help to balance out their behavior a lot, and can bring in some more calm to the whole household. In addition, when the other people in the home can be calm and collected around the pet, this can translate into the personality of your pet as well, making life so much easier.

With this in mind, it is time to look at a few of the other things that you are going to be able to do in order to handle your pet and actually enjoy them, rather than worrying about them being too active or adding more stress in your life. The first thing that you can do here is to get out and enjoy nature with your pet. This is especially important if you have to spend some time at work; your pet may feel a bit neglected during those long absences.

Spending a bit of time on a walk or outside with your pet helps you both to enjoy nature and allows you to get some fresh air at the same time. Walking your dog is a great activity for both of you because it helps you and the pet bond, gets you outside into the fresh air, and can encourage you to be more active. The dog or cat (or ferret, or whatever) is also going to enjoy this because they get to spend time with you, while also burning off some of that extra energy they have from being stuck inside all day.

Now, there are times when a dog or another pet you are dealing with is going to run into some behavioral problems; this is to be expected. If this is something that you have been dealing with in your pet - especially when it comes to destroying items and chewing on things they should not - most therapists that work with pet behavior will encourage you to start out by walking the dog on a daily basis, right when you get home if possible.

The reason that this is going to be so successful is that often the dog is acting out because either they want some more attention to you, or they want to be able to get out some of the excess energy that they have from being trapped inside all day long. The walk is going to help with both or either of these two problems, and you will be surprised at how much of a difference this is going to make in how well your pet behaves.

If you are working with a cat that stays indoors or another kind of pet that is not able to go outside, there are still steps that you are able to take to ensure that this pet gets a bit more nature in its life. For example, if you have a fish tank, or another container with a turtle, snake, or lizard living inside of it, you could do some research to find plants that are safe for your pet and can be put into the tank. This is a safe and effective manner to bring some of outside nature into your pet's surroundings.

Let us say that your pet is a rodent and they are not able to head outside or enjoy any soil or plants; try opening up a window that is near them for at least a bit each day so they can get some fresh air. Just make sure that you are not trying to do this when it is too cold outside, or when there might be a chance that the pet is able to escape out of the window and go exploring on their own outside without you.

Just like with the other parts that come with lagom, you have to remember to always practice balance, especially when it comes to the choice about whether or not you should bring home a new pet to your family. Some people find that this is *just enough* to complete their family and make things so much better and happier. On the other hand, some others find that it is just too much work and stress for them. If you want to bring home a pet because it seems like the right choice for you, then go ahead and do that. However, if you are bringing home a pet because you feel that you are obligated to, or because everyone else has one, then this is not lagom. In this case, it is best to leave well enough alone.

Also, if you are a big animal lover and feel a big tug on your heartstrings to take in every needy or stray animal that you see, be aware that this is not lagom. It may be a noble thing to do and shows your big heart, but it is going to be stressful and too much. Caring for all of those animals is not going to be the *just enough* that lagom is trying to promote! Also, consider that this is going to cause such an imbalance as your home gets taken over by clutter, destroyed by animals, and overrun in a manner that you cannot control. This does not sound relaxing at all!

While having a pet is a perfect way to add to your family and can certainly be the way that you add some more lagom into your life, it isn't necessarily something that you want to go overboard with. For some people, it is something that you don't want to do at all. Learning what is best for your family, and having just enough in terms of pets (whether this is none, one, or more) can make a difference; they must fit in with the lagom lifestyle that you are trying to build.

Chapter 13: Lagom While Traveling

Another topic that we are going to spend a little bit of time discussing when it comes to lagom is the idea of how lagom can work when it comes to traveling. Many people love to travel. Whether it is a quick visit to go and see a family member or a friend, or something that is meant to be a vacation with the kids, or on your own, to some place that is new and exciting, a vacation can be something that we can implement into the process of lagom.

Planning a vacation is sometimes going to be a mixed bag. We are excited about the journey and where we are going, but trying to plan all of the details, such as where you should stay, what to see, how to get there, what to eat, and more can be a big hassle sometimes. Planning all of this and coming up with a budget to cover it all - especially if you are taking yourself and the kids - can give you a headache and often makes you wonder if it is worth the trouble and the stress in the first place.

The good news is that you are able to do the traveling and create all of those great memories at the same time! Let's dive in and see some of the steps that you can take in order to make this happen while maintaining your lagom lifestyle.

Taking a vacation from work can be a good thing because it helps to create more of a healthy work-to-life balance, and for many people, it turns into an extremely relaxing experience. On the other hand, as we discussed a bit before, it can take a lot of planning and execution in order to make the vacation all work out, especially if it is to a location that you have not been to in the past. All of this comes together to be extremely stressful in the process.

Traveling, depending on the methods that you use to do so, can be a strenuous time for not only you, but for the whole family. Remember, the whole point of this is to have some time together, to take a break, and even to bond with one another along the way. This is what every family wants when they decide to travel together and have some fun, but sometimes, the plans aren't always going to work the way that we think they should, and this can create a lot of anxiety, discontent, and - of course - anger in the process. The idea of lagom, if it is used in the proper manner, can help to fix all of these problems and give you the family vacation that you are dreaming about.

Practicing lagom throughout your travels, as well as the whole time that you are actually traveling, can help you to stay more focused, help you to relax, and ensures that you are able to keep some of the mindfulness in your life as well. When you are able to bring all of these different parts together at the same time, they help you to form some stronger and longer-lasting memories of the experience and the vacation as well. Some of the tips that you can use to help make your travels more fun and relaxing while adding in some lagom to the experience are discussed below.

Make some plans to help you stay organized, but do not stress out if you are not able to stick to them exactly for one reason or another. Things are going to happen in life, and no matter how well you plan and try to keep on schedule things are not always going to turn out the way that you would like. If you do not add in some flexibility to the plans, then you are going to end up with grumpy kids, anxiety in you, lots of fighting, and so on, just because of a little shift in plans.

For example, be sure to plan ahead in terms of scheduling the transportation that you want to take to get to your destination, such as a train a bus or a plane. You should also take some time to plan ahead to figure out where you are going to stay the night, such as which hotel you are going to use when you do get to your destination.

However, even these things are going to change. The plane may take off late and you will not be able to get to your destination at the time you had planned. Alternatively, you may find that the hotel you wanted to be booked up too fast and you now need to make some changes to get to the right location and have a place to sleep. Stressing out about this because it goes against your plans is not going to be a good idea and can start to taint some of the good memories that you are trying to make. No matter how hard you try, things are not always going to work the way you want, and you will have a much more enjoyable time if you can take a step back and relax, rather than feeling dark and disappointed because things did not work out.

Outside of some of the necessities that we talked about above, try to keep most of the schedule loose and flexible. You can go and do some things as you would like to but realize that you don't need to be there at a certain time; leave things open in case someone is tired and needs a break. It is also a good idea to allow some downtime in the day, just hanging by the pool or at the hotel room, so that you are not rushing around the whole time.

Now, there may be times when you want to leave the country to do some of your own exploring and to have more of an adventure when you travel. Before you go, maybe consider bonding with your whole family as you try to learn a few keywords and phrases that will work in that country and in their language. You can also try out new foods in the area and visit some of the important landmarks while you are there

Always make sure that you are practicing the right kind of balance, and make sure that everyone in the party is respectful when it comes to visiting with cultures that are outside your own. You may not fully understand why a culture would want to take part in one practice, or why they like a certain food or holiday, but you can still learn how to be respectful and learn about their culture, rather than causing problems.

If you plan to head out to a destination that is going to be pretty hectic the whole time, such as a major theme park or a beach that is pretty busy, then you should also plan some time to take it easy and relax into your day. If you can, set aside time when everyone can get away from the hustle and bustle and take a nap as they wish, or even have them just sit down and read or listen to their favorite music rather than having all of that stimulation.

Yes, being at a theme park can be a lot of fun, and there are always a million things that you are going to be able to do while you are there. However, these experiences can have so much stimulation that i puts you out of balance, and your energy levels are going to deplete so quickly - much faster than they will do at home. Having this break to recharge is going to be a great way to balance yourself out again after all that noise, those sights, and everything else that is out in the amusement park. Taking small breaks can help you to feel better and ready to take on more during the day.

It is also possible to take a vacation that is meant to just be relaxing and nothing else. You may assume that to go on a vacation you need to be out there, planning a ton of activities and running around the whole time to get the good memories. However, this is just not the case. It is going to end up causing you a lot of stress and headaches, and while it is sometimes fun to have a good plan, other times it is nice to just take a vacation, sit back, and relax during it.

Never underestimate the idea that it can be vital and so important for you to just spend some time together om a new location, with some different scenery, rather than having to be home all the time. Even planning a big vacation can cause a lot of stress! Consider renting a big cabin in the woods together and hanging out with your extended family. Alternatively, maybe hit the beach and just have fun with the water and the sand and something good to eat and drink along the way.

These are just a few examples of what you can do when dealing with a true lagom experience when you go on a vacation. There are too many families who are trying to make things perfect and planning every part of the whole vacation. While this may be done with good intentions along the way, it is not going to encourage the fun and the bonding that these trips are supposed to have, simply because it causes too much stress and too much anxiety on the whole family. Let go a bit, just be flexible, and realize that the most important thing to do here is to just spend time with your family and have some fun. If you can do this, then you are well on your way to having a vacation that is balanced, fun, and going to help you to create some great memories.

Going on a vacation with your family does not have to be a lot of work or hard or anything like that. It is meant to help you to have fun and take a break from all of the work and other obligations that you meet on a regular basis. A vacation helps you to create the bonds and the memories that you want with your children as they grow up. With the help of lagom and some of the different options that we have talked about in this chapter, you will be able to take some of the stress out of your vacation planning so you can actually have a good time.

Conclusion

Thank for making it through to the end of *lagom*, let us hope it was informative, providing you with all the tools you need to achieve your goals - whatever they may be.

The next step is to decide how you would like to implement the ideas of lagom that we have discussed in this guidebook. There are so many different ways that you are able to do this! Learning the right steps, and how to make them work for you, can take some time and some dedication. However, with a good plan in place - and possibly starting with one step at a time – you can make this happen and live a life that you deeply enjoy.

The ideas of lagom are not groundbreaking - or even that hard to do. However, we live in a society where consumerism is the norm and where people are always competing to buy the latest thing and to own more of what they do not really need. This leads to a lot of clutter, a lot of extra work that is not needed; it also leads to a country full of people with no friends, too much work, and a lot of stress, and stuff that does not make them happy at all.

If you are tired of this kind of lifestyle and you are looking for a way to reduce the stress, improve your mental and physical wellbeing, and to ensure that you are getting the most out of your life, then lagom may be the answer for you. In addition, this guidebook has spent some time looking at the various steps that you can take in order to get this done.

When you are ready to simplify your life, ensure that you are gaining more happiness and enjoyment out of your life than ever before, and simplify your life all at the same time, make sure to check out this guidebook to help you get started with lagom.

Finally, if you found this book useful in any way, a review on Amazon is always appreciated!

Made in the USA
Monee, IL
17 December 2019

19006168R00116